KNIT AND FELT BAGS

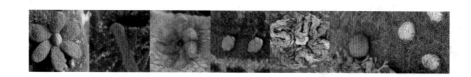

st

KNIT AND FELT BAGS

20 QUICK-AND-EASY EMBELLISHED BAGS

BEV BEATTIE

First published in Great Britain in 2009 by
A&C Black Publishers Ltd
36 Soho Square
London W1D 3QY
www.acblack.com

Photography: **Sussie Bell**
Design: **Elizabeth Healey**
Commissioning editor:
  Janet Ravenscroft
Project manager: **Kate Haxell**

This book was conceived and produced by Breslich & Foss Ltd, London

A CIP catalogue record for this book is available from the British Library

ISBN 978 1 408 11553 4

Printed and bound in China

10 9 8 7 6 5 4 3

contents

Introduction   6

Bucket bags   8
Pure purple   10
Plant pot   14
Flower power   18
Paint box bag   22

Flat-bottomed bags   28
Jazzy bag   30
Orange fluff and bobble   36
Anything goes stash bag   40
Retro button bag   46
Slip stitch honeycomb   50

Variegated stripe bag	86
Half bobble bag	92
Violets are blue	96
Small floral bag	102
Pom-pom perfect	106

Shaped bags	**54**
Red wool and ribbon	56
Cherry ripe	60
Recycled sari silk bag	66
Little saddle bag	72
Acorn and oak leaf	76
Monochrome jazz	82

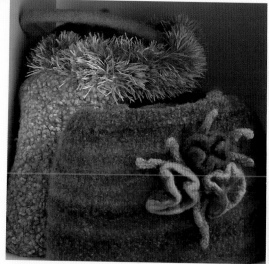

Yarns and techniques	110
Abbreviations	125
Conversions	125
Resources	126
Index	127
Acknowledgements	128

introduction

I discovered felting when a friend gave me some very thick pure wool, almost like a roving. I had to knit this wool on very thick needles, like broom handles, and this very large bag started to appear. Then came the exciting bit: I put it in the washing machine. I found myself standing waiting for the washing machine to finish – how crazy is that!

When I opened the washing machine door, this very large bag that I thought would hold my big college portfolio had become a shallow knitting-needle bag. Not being a person to let this go, I made another one, and another one, until I had a bag of the correct proportions. I loved it, but by then the wool had run out.

I bought various pure wool yarns, or so-called pure wools. I found that many of these wools had been treated chemically or were super-wash wool and so they would not felt. That is where the wonders of the Internet came into play. I sourced wool yarns from all over the world, found the perfect yarn for what I wanted and started to make more and more bags. There was no going back now.

I took a few bags into college to show my classmates and one of the students, Jenny, wanted to buy a bag. I was absolutely stunned when she offered me the money there and then. A few days later another lady, Tanya, wanted to buy a different bag and I realised that maybe these bags could sell.

The secret is in the wool yarn: if you have good wool, the bags work.

My mum, Doreen, and my sisters, Bridget and Bernadette, took my bags to their friends, work, hairdressers and many other places. They were great sales staff and I was selling bags as fast as I could knit them. I was buying kilos of yarn and friends at college asked to buy that, too, and that is where my yarn business, Knitting4fun, started.

Soon after that I attended a knitting and stitching show and, realising that I could not knit enough bags to keep up with the demand, I made up a few kits with the wool yarns, needles and pattern needed to make the bags. These all sold and each evening after the show I had to make up more and more kits. My husband, Tom, and his friend, David, built my website and the business grew. This is why we now have yarn in every room of the house, except the bathroom (you could get a lot of yarn in that bath though!)

The great thing about knitting and felting is that it's quick and easy to do and is very forgiving. Once the knitting is felted you cannot see that your tension isn't perfect, that you may have dropped a stitch, or any other small mistakes in the knitting. Beginners and the more experienced alike will get excellent results.

The secret is in the wool yarn: if you have good wool, the bags work. I use my own Knitting4fun wool yarns, which I know felt at 40 degrees in the washing machine. You'll find information on these yarns, and ideas for substitute yarns, on pages 112–118.

I hope you enjoy knitting and felting your own bags as much as I do.

Bev Beattie

Once the knitting is felted you cannot see that your tension isn't perfect, that you may have dropped a stitch, or any other small mistakes in the knitting.

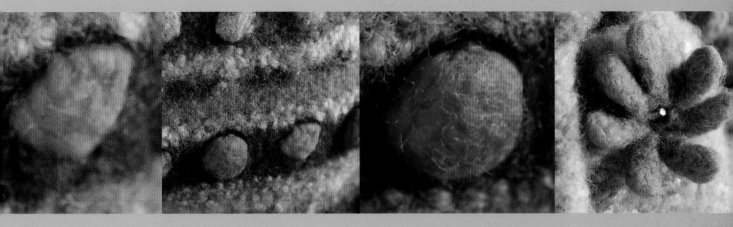

bucket
bags

This style of bag is very simple and quick to knit –
perfect for novice knitters to try. The bucket shape
works well with longer handles that you can sling over
your shoulder, so the bags are practical carry-alls as
well as stylish accessories.

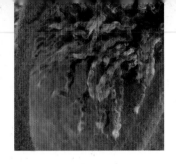

pure purple

You will need

- 125g of Knitting4fun Pure Wool in Purple (A)
- 50g of Elle Pizzazz in Poison 252 (B)
- 125g of Knitting4fun Pure Wool in Damson (C)
- 8mm (60cm/24 in. long) circular needle
- 10mm (60cm/24 in. or 80cm/32 in. long) circular needle
- Set of five 10mm double-pointed needles
- Knitter's sewing needle or bodkin for sewing
- Large snap fastener or press stud (optional)

Finished size

Bag measures approx 24cm/9½ in. high by 23cm/9 in. wide.

This was one of the first bags I ever made. I love the Elle Pizzazz yarn and wanted to use it to make a dramatically textured bag.

The shape of this bag was originally inspired by a hat pattern: imagine it upside down and smaller! The revised pattern is so easy to knit and can be adapted to make a bag of any size, small or large.

This bag was made with two different shades of purple yarn knitted together to give a slightly variegated effect. This complements the mix of colours in the textured yarn making the wonderful fringe around the top of the bag.

The decreases for the bottom of the bag are made on double-pointed needles. Knitted i-cord handles complete the bag and these can be knitted almost any length to suit your needs.

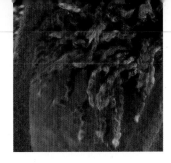

Tension

12 stitches and 14 rows to 10cm/4 in. over st st on 10mm needles using two strands of A held together, although tension is not crucial in felting.

Abbreviations

See page 125.

Bag

Using 8mm circular needle and one strand each of A and B held together, cast on 65 sts.

Join the cast on row into a circle, ensuring that the knitting is not twisted, and place a marker to establish the beginning of the round.

Purl 8 to 10 rounds, or until the trim at the top of the bag is the desired depth. Purling the stitches helps to keep the textured yarn on the right side of the knitting. Tease out the long fibres as you work so that they do not get trapped in the knitted fabric.

Break off B and join in a strand of C.

Change to 10mm circular needle and cont in knit stitch.

Next round: [K12, inc] five times. (70 sts)

Knit 45 rounds using one strand each of A and C held together.

Shape base

Slip marker to the right-hand needle and start the shaping as folls:

Next round: [K8, k2tog] to the end of the round. (63 sts)

Knit 3 rounds.

Next round: [K7, k2tog] to the end of the round. (56 sts)

Knit 2 rounds.

Change to 10mm double-pointed needles as folls:

Next round: *[K6, k2tog] twice onto one double-pointed needle; rep from * onto two more needles then k6, k2tog once onto the fourth needle. (49 sts)

Cont shaping on double-pointed needles as folls:

Knit 1 round.

Next round: [K5, k2tog] to the end of the round. (42 sts)

Next round: [K4, k2tog] to the end of the round. (35 sts)

Next round: [K3, k2tog] to the end of the round. (28 sts)

Next round: [K2, k2tog] to the end of the round. (21 sts)

Next round: [K1, k2tog] to the end of the round. (14 sts)

Next round: [K2tog] to the end of the round. (7 sts)

Leaving a 40cm/15 in. tail, cut yarn. Thread tail through rem sts. Thread tail into knitter's sewing needle and sew through these sts several times to secure the end.

Handles (make two)

Using 10mm double-pointed needles and two strands of A held together (or one strand each of A and C held together if you prefer), cast on 4 sts.

Knit 1 row.

Switch needles in your hands, so the needle with the stitches on is in your left hand again. Slide the stitches to the other end of the needle and, pulling the yarn across the back of the stitches, knit the row again. The first three or four rows will be flat but don't worry, after that the knitting will become tubular. Before knitting the first stitch of each row, give the yarn a tug to make the strand across the back disappear.

Cont in this way, sliding and knitting, until the handle is the required length. As the handles will shrink by approximately one-third during felting, I usually knit about 50–60 rows for a short hand-held handle, 100 rows for a longer hand-held handle and 120–140 rows for a shoulder handle.

Cast off.

To make up

Using the knitter's sewing needle and A, sew the handles to the inside of the trim section at the top of the bag, about 1.5cm/½ in. down from the top edge.

Darn in all loose ends.

Following the instructions on pages 123–124, machine-wash the bag to felt it.

You can sew on a large snap fastener or press stud to fasten the bag if desired.

This bag was made with two different shades of purple yarn knitted together to give a slightly variegated effect. This complements the mix of colours in the textured yarn making the wonderful fringe around the top of the bag.

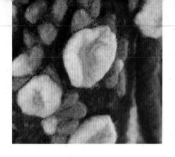

plant pot

The lovingly tended potted plants in my mother's garden inspired me to design this bag. The mixture of the rust-coloured pure wool yarn and the variegated ribbon yarn gives the look of the weathering on her terracotta pots.

Small sprays of knitted leaves tumble down the sides of the bag, with crocheted buds and flowers growing from them. Add a couple of leaves and flowers to the handles, too, for a finishing touch. This pattern can be made with flowers in any colours to make a very pretty and dainty bag.

The bag can be made without a handle and used as a plant pot holder. It would be lovely with flowers crocheted in colours to match the potted plant placed in it, or to co-ordinate with your room décor.

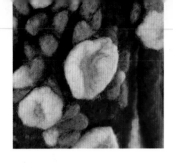

Tension

14 stitches and 16 rows to
10cm/4 in. over st st on 9mm
needles using one strand
each of A and B held
together, although tension is
not crucial in felting.

Abbreviations

See page 125.

Bag

Using 8mm circular needle and one strand each of A and B held together, cast on
55 sts.

Join the cast on row into a circle, ensuring that the knitting is not twisted, and
place a marker to establish the beginning of the round.

Round 1: [K1, p1] to last st, k1.

Round 2: [P1, k1] to last st, p1.

Rep rounds 1–2 once more then rep round 1 once more.

Round 6: [K10, inc] five times. (60 sts)

Change to 9mm circular needle and cont in knit stitch.

Knit 35 rounds.

Shape base

Slip marker to the right-hand needle and start the shaping as folls:

Round 42: [K8, k2tog] to the end of the round. (54 sts)

Knit 2 rounds.

Round 45: [K7, k2tog] to the end of the round. (48 sts)

Knit 2 rounds.

Change to 9mm double-pointed needles as folls:

Round 48: *[K6, k2tog] twice onto one double-pointed needle; rep from * onto two
more needles. (42 sts)

Cont shaping on double-pointed needles as folls:

Knit 1 round.

Round 50: [K5, k2tog] to the end of the round. (36 sts)

Round 51: [K4, k2tog] to the end of the round. (30 sts)

Round 52: [K3, k2tog] to the end of the round. (24 sts)

Round 53: [K2, k2tog] to the end of the round. (18 sts)

Round 54: [K1, k2tog] to the end of the round. (12 sts)

Round 55: [K2tog] to the end of the round. (6 sts)

Leaving a 40cm/15 in. tail, cut yarn. Thread tail through rem sts. Thread tail into
knitter's sewing needle and sew through these sts several times to secure the end.

Handle (make one)

Using 9mm double-pointed needles and one strand of A, cast on 4 sts.

Knit 1 row.

Switch needles in your hands, so the needle with the stitches on is in your left hand
again. Slide the stitches to the other end of the needle and, pulling the yarn across
the back of the stitches, knit the row again. The first three or four rows will be flat but

don't worry, after that the knitting will become tubular. Before knitting the first stitch of each row, give the yarn a tug to make the strand across the back disappear.

Cont in this way, sliding and knitting, until the handle is the required length. As the handles will shrink by approximately one-third during felting, I usually knit about 50–60 rows for a short hand-held handle, 100 rows for a longer hand-held handle and 120–140 rows for a shoulder handle.

Cast off.

Trailing leaves

Using 6mm knitting needles and one strand of Apple Green Pure Wool, cast on 7 sts.

Row 1: *Cast off 6 sts, slip rem st onto the left-hand needle and cast on 6 sts; rep from * to make a long chain of leaves. Vary the length of the leaves by casting on more or fewer sts, always casting off until 1 st is left.

When chain is desired length, fasten off.

Crochet flower

Using 6mm crochet hook and one strand of Yellow Pure Wool, ch 5, join with a slip st to form a ring.

Change to Cream Pure Wool and make 10 dc in ring.

Join.

Ch 3, make 3 tr in next st, chain 2, dc in next st.

Repeat from * to * around ring four more times to make five petals.

Fasten off, leaving a 50cm/20 in. tail.

To make up

Drape the chain of trailing leaves around the bag and sew it in place using the knitter's sewing needle and matching yarn.

Using matching yarn, sew the flowers in place.

Using A, sew the handle to the inside of the top of the bag, about 1.5cm/½ in. down from the top edge.

Darn in all loose ends.

Following the instructions on pages 123–124, machine-wash the bag to felt it.

You can sew on a large snap fastener or press stud to fasten the bag if desired.

flower power

You will need

- 150g of Knitting4fun
  Pure Wool in
  Lime Green (A)
- 100g of Colinette Giotto
  in Lagoon 138 (B)
- Small amount of
  Knitting4fun Pure Wool in
  Turquoise (C)
- Beads for embellishing
  flowers
- 8mm (40cm/16 in.
  or 60cm/24 in. long)
  circular needle
- 9mm (40cm/24 in. long)
  circular needle
- Set of four 9mm
  double-pointed needles
- 4mm crochet hook
- Pair of 6mm
  knitting needles
- Knitter's sewing needle or
  bodkin for sewing
- Large snap fastener or
  press stud (optional)

Finished size

Bag measures approx
22cm/8½ in. high by
22cm/8½ in. wide.

While on holiday a few years ago, I found in a local shop a small lavender bag made from silk. It was meant to be hung in the wardrobe, but I thought it was too beautiful to be hidden away. It was that bag that inspired this one.

I decided to make this bag in two of my favourite colours – lime-green and turquoise. The clean, fresh colours evoke the summer and sunshine for me and remind me of my trips abroad.

I love the way that the wool yarn felts with the ribbon yarns, giving a sheen to the surface of the bag. Crystal beads sewn into the centres of the small turquoise flowers add a little sparkle.

Make this pattern as a bag or as a holder filled with your favourite pot pourri to hang in your room.

Bag

Using 8mm circular needle and one strand each of A and B held together, cast on 55 sts.

Join the cast on row into a circle, ensuring that the knitting is not twisted, and place a marker to establish the beginning of the round.

Round 1: [K1, p1] to last st, k1.

Round 2: [P1, k1] to last st, p1.

Rep rounds 1–2 once more then rep round 1 once more.

Round 6: [K10, inc] five times. (60 sts)

Change to 9mm circular needle and cont in knit stitch.

Knit 35 rounds.

Shape base

Slip marker to the right-hand needle and start the shaping as folls:

Round 42: [K8, k2tog] to the end of the round. (54 sts)

Knit 2 rounds.

Round 45: [K7, k2tog] to the end of the round. (48 sts)

Knit 2 rounds.

Change to 9mm double-pointed needles as folls:

Round 48: *[K6, k2tog] twice onto one double-pointed needle; rep from * onto two more needles. (42 sts)

Cont shaping on double-pointed needles as folls:

Knit 1 round.

Round 50: [K5, k2tog] to the end of the round. (36 sts)

Round 51: [K4, k2tog] to the end of the round. (30 sts)

Round 52: [K3, k2tog] to the end of the round. (24 sts)

Round 53: [K2, k2tog] to the end of the round. (18 sts)

Round 54: [K1, k2tog] to the end of the round. (12 sts)

Round 55: [K2tog] to the end of the round. (6 sts)

Leaving a 40cm/15 in. tail, cut yarn. Thread tail through rem sts. Thread tail into knitter's sewing needle and sew through these sts several times to secure the end.

Handle (make one)

Using 9mm double-pointed needles and one strand of A, cast on 4 sts.

Knit 1 row.

Switch needles in your hands, so the needle with the stitches on is in your left hand again. Slide the stitches to the other end of the needle and, pulling the yarn across the back of the stitches, knit the row again. The first three or four rows will be flat but don't worry, after that the knitting will become tubular. Before knitting the first stitch of each row, give the yarn a tug to make the strand across the back disappear. Cont in this way, sliding and knitting, until the handle is the required length. As the handles will shrink by approximately one-third during felting, I usually knit about 50–60 rows for a short hand-held handle, 100 rows for a longer hand-held handle and 120–140 rows for a shoulder handle.

Cast off.

Using the 4mm crochet hook and C, work a chain the same length as the knitted i-cord handle.

Daisy

Using 6mm knitting needles and one strand of C, cast on 7 sts.

Row 1: *Cast off 6 sts, slip rem st onto the left-hand needle and cast on 6 sts; rep from * five or six times more, depending on number of petals required. Leaving a 50cm/20 in. tail, fasten off last st. Using matching yarn, sew the beginning and end together to join into a circle. Gather the centre by threading the tail into the knitter's sewing needle and sewing along the straight edge and pulling tight. Sew through these sts several times to secure the end. Do not cut the tail.

Sew a bead into the centre of each flower.

To make up

Using the tail of yarn attached to each flower, sew the flowers in place.

Twist the knitted and crocheted handle cords together and, using A, sew the ends to the inside of the top of the bag, about 1.5cm/½ in. down from the top edge.

Darn in all loose ends.

Following the instructions on pages 123–124, machine-wash the bag to felt it.

You can sew on a large snap fastener or press stud to fasten the bag if desired.

The clean, fresh colours evoke the summer and sunshine for me and remind me of my trips abroad.

paint box bag

You will need

- 400g in total of Knitting4fun Pure Wool consisting of small amounts of Black (A), Sunshine Yellow (B), Purple (C), Orange (D), Bright Green (E), Red (F), Royal Blue (G), Turquoise (H), Dark Green (I), Fuchsia Pink (J) and Lime Green (K)
- 8mm (60cm/24 in. long) circular needle
- 10mm (80cm/32 in. long) circular needle
- Set of five 10mm double-pointed needles
- Knitter's sewing needle or bodkin for sewing
- Large snap fastener or press stud (optional)

Finished size

Bag measures approx 28cm/11 in. high by 30cm/12 in. wide.

On a cold, dreary weekend in winter I bought a paint box and crayon set to keep the children busy. The set included a mosaic-style colouring book that the children filled in with cheerful, bright colours and it was that which got me thinking about this bag.

I did not plan the colours, I just knitted them as they came to me: it was quite a freeform project. I made the bobbles as I was knitting the bag, but also added more texture by embroidering French knots afterwards, as I decided I wanted more contrast colours in some areas.

I had initially thought of adding brightly coloured buttons on some of the stripes, but after I had made the bobbles and added the embroidery, I decided that I would leave the buttons for another bag.

Tension

12 stitches and 14 rows to 10cm/4 in. over st st on 10mm needles using two strands of A held together, although tension is not crucial in felting.

Abbreviations

MB = make bobble: in contrast colour (k1, p1, k1) into next st, turn p3, turn k3, turn p3, turn sk2po, slip the stitch back onto the left-hand needle and knit into it again using main colour; cut contrast yarn, pull ends of contrast yarn tight to form the bobble, knot ends together and sew them into the back of the bobble before felting. See also page 125.

Note: use two strands of yarn held together throughout unless otherwise stated. Cut yarns between stripes and sew ends in before felting.

Bag

Using 8mm circular needle and two strands of A, cast on 75 sts.

Join the cast on row into a circle, ensuring that the knitting is not twisted, and place a marker to establish the beginning of the round.

Round 1: [K1, p1] to last st, k1.

Round 2: [P1, k1] to last st, p1.

Rep rounds 1–2 twice more.

Round 7: [K14, inc] five times. (80 sts)

Change to 10mm circular needle and cont in knit stitch.

Knit 2 rounds in B.

Round 10 (bobble round): [K7 in B, MB in C] to the end of the round.

Knit 2 rounds in B.

Knit 3 rounds in D.

Round 16: [K4 in E, sl 1 st in D] to the end of the round.

Rep round 16 once more.

Knit 2 rounds in E.

Knit 2 rounds in F.

Round 22: In F [k7, M1] to the end of the round. (90 sts)

Knit 3 rounds in G.

Round 26 (bobble round): [K4 in G, MB in H] to the end of the round.

Knit 3 rounds in G.

Knit 3 rounds in B.

Round 33: [K4 in I, sl 1 st in B] to the end of the round.

Rep round 33 once more.

Knit 3 rounds in J.

Knit 2 rounds in K.

Round 40: In C [k9, M1] to the end of the round. (100 sts)

Knit 2 rounds in C.

Round 43 (bobble round): *K4 in C, MB in F, k4 in C, MB with one strand of D; rep from * to the end of the round.

Knit 2 rounds in C.

Knit 3 rounds in H.

Knit 3 rounds in B.

Round 52: [K4 in J, sl 1 st in B] to the end of the round.

Knit 3 rounds in I.

Knit 2 rounds in E.

Round 58 (bobble round): [K9 in E, MB in L] to the end of the round.

Knit 1 round in E.

Shape base

Slip marker to the right-hand needle and start the shaping as folls:

Round 60: In E [k8, k2tog] to the end of the round. (90 sts)

Knit 3 rounds in K.

Round 64: [K2 in C, sl 1 st in K] to the end of the round.

Rep round 64 twice more.

Knit 1 round in J.

Round 68: In J [k7, k2tog] to the end of the round. (80 sts)

Knit 1 round in G.

Change to 10mm double-pointed needles as folls:

Round 70: *[K6, k2tog] three times onto one double-pointed needle; rep from * onto one more needle, **[K6, k2tog] twice onto next double-pointed needle; rep from ** onto last needle. (70 sts)

Cont shaping on double-pointed needles as folls:

Knit 1 round in G.

Round 72: In F [k5, k2tog] to the end of the round. (60 sts)

Knit 1 round in F.

Round 74: In B [k4, k2tog] to the end of the round. (50 sts)

Knit 1 round in B.

Round 76: In G [k3, k2tog] to the end of the round. (40 sts)

Round 77: In G [k2, k2tog] to the end of the round. (30 sts)

Round 78: In K [k1, k2tog] to the end of the round. (20 sts)

Round 79: In K [k2tog] to the end of the round. (10 sts)

Leaving a 40cm/15 in. tail, cut yarn. Thread tail through rem sts. Thread tail into knitter's sewing needle and sew through these sts several times to secure the end.

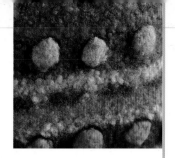

I did not plan the colours, I just knitted them as they came to me: it was quite a freeform project.

Handles (make two)

Using 10mm double-pointed needles and two strands of A held together, cast on 5 sts.
Knit 1 row.

Switch needles in your hands, so the needle with the stitches on is in your left hand again. Slide the stitches to the other end of the needle and, pulling the yarn across the back of the stitches, knit the row again. The first three or four rows will be flat but don't worry, after that the knitting will become tubular. Before knitting the first stitch of each row, give the yarn a tug to make the strand across the back disappear.

Cont in this way, sliding and knitting, until the handle is the required length. As the handles will shrink by approximately one-third during felting, I usually knit about 50–60 rows for a short hand-held handle, 100 rows for a longer hand-held handle and 120–140 rows for a shoulder handle.

Cast off.

To make up

Using the knitter's sewing needle and yarns of your choice, add embroidery stitches such as French knots (the small dots on this bag) to the knitting.

Using the knitter's sewing needle and A, sew the handles to the inside of the top of the bag, about 1.5cm/½ in. down from the top edge.

Darn in all loose ends.

Following the instructions on pages 123–124, machine-wash the bag to felt it.

You can sew on a large snap fastener or press stud to fasten the bag if desired.

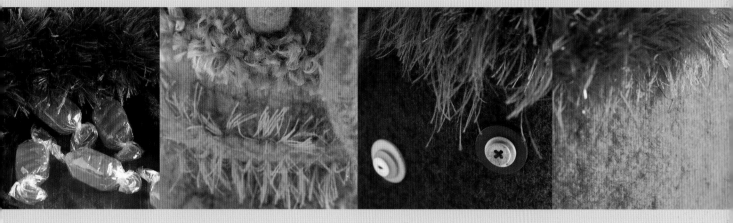

flat-bottomed bags

These bags use a three-needle cast-off to close
the base seam and so complete them. Once felted,
this cast off is almost invisible, making your bag
appear seamless.

jazzy bag

The fabulous, bright, 'jazzy' colours in this bag make it one of my favourites. I love the dreadlock-style fringe that the Elle Pizzazz yarn produces, and this colourway works so well with the turquoise wool yarn I chose for the main body of the bag. The pink eyelash yarn mixed in with the Pizzazz adds colour contrast and thickens out the fringe beautifully.

The Pizzazz yarn comes in lots of different colour combinations and I must have knitted versions of this bag using most of them, as they are all so gorgeous.

If you want to try a different colour combination to the one I've used here, just choose a wool yarn from the Knitting4fun range that matches one of the strand colours in the Pizzazz. The Ice Long Eyelash yarn is also available in lots of colours, so you can mix-and-match to create your own unique combination.

The book bag version of this pattern (see page 34) will hold lots of paperwork and is far more stylish than a briefcase. It'll also hold a laptop and the thick yarn provides extra padding.

Tension

12 stitches and 14 rows to 10cm/4 in. over st st on 10mm needles using two strands of A held together, although tension is not crucial in felting.

Abbreviations

See page 125.

Bag

Using 8mm circular needle and one strand each of A, B and C held together, cast on 65 sts.

   *Join the cast on row into a circle, ensuring that the knitting is not twisted, and place a marker to establish the beginning of the round.

   Purl 7 to 9 rounds, or until the trim at the top of the bag is the desired depth. Purling the stitches helps to keep the textured yarn on the right side of the knitting. Tease out the long fibres as you work so that they do not get trapped in the knitted fabric.*

   Break off B and C and join in another strand of A.

Next round: [K12, inc] five times. (70 sts)

   Change to 10mm circular needle and cont in knit stitch.

   Knit 45 rounds using two strands of A held together.

Shape base

Slip marker to the right-hand needle and start the shaping as folls:

Next round: K5, k2tog, k21, k2togtbl, k10, k2tog, k21, k2togtbl, k5. (66 sts)

Next round: K4, k2tog, k21, k2togtbl, k8, k2tog, k21, k2togtbl, k4. (62 sts)

Next round: K3, k2tog, k21, k2togtbl, k6, k2tog, k21, k2togtbl, k3. (58 sts)

Next round: K2, k2tog, k21, k2togtbl, k4, k2tog, k21, k2togtbl, k2. (54 sts)

Next round: K1, k2tog, k21, k2togtbl, k2, k2tog, k21, k2togtbl, k1. (50 sts)

Next round: K2tog, k21, k2togtbl, k2tog, k21, k2togtbl. (46 sts)

**Join base

Turn the bag inside out and push 23 sts along to each needle point. Put both needle points together and, using another knitting needle (the same size as the circular needle or a size larger), knit tog the first st on each needle point. Knit tog the second st on each needle point, then slip the first st over the second st, so casting off (not too tightly) and joining the base of the bag at the same time. Rep until all sts are cast off.

Handles (make two)

Using 10mm double-pointed needles and two strands of A held together, cast on 4 sts.

   Knit 1 row.

   Switch needles in your hands, so the needle with the stitches on is in your left hand again. Slide the stitches to the other end of the needle and, pulling the yarn across the back of the stitches, knit the row again. The first three or four rows will be flat but don't worry, after that the knitting will become tubular. Before knitting the first stitch of each row, give the yarn a tug to make the strand across the back disappear.

Cont in this way, sliding and knitting, until the handle is the required length. As the handles will shrink by approximately one-third during felting, I usually knit about 50–60 rows for a short hand-held handle, 100 rows for a longer hand-held handle and 120–140 rows for a shoulder handle.

Cast off.

To make up

Using the knitter's sewing needle and A, sew the handles to the inside of the trim section at the top of the bag, about 1.5cm/½ in. down from the top edge.

Darn in all loose ends.

Following the instructions on pages 123–124, machine-wash the bag to felt it.

You can sew on a large snap fastener or press stud to fasten the bag if desired.

The Pizzazz yarn comes in lots of different colours and I must have knitted versions of this bag using most of them, as they are all so gorgeous.

jazzy book bag

You will need

- 400g of Knitting4fun
  Pure Wool in Turquoise (A)
- 50g of Filati FF Park in
  colour 45 (B)
- 200g of Ice Catena in
  Aqua/Green/Blue (C)

Finished size

Bag measures approx
27cm/10½ in. high by
36cm/14 in. wide.

Bag

Using 8mm circular needle and one strand each of A and B held together, cast on
100 sts.

Follow Jazzy Bag pattern from * to *.

Break off B and join in a strand of C.

Next round: [K9, inc] ten times. (110 sts)

Change to 10mm circular needle and cont in knit stitch.

Knit 65 rounds.

Shape base

Slip marker to the right-hand needle and start the shaping as folls:

Next round: K7, k2tog, k41, k2togtbl, k14, k2tog, k41, k2togtbl, k7. (106 sts)

Next round: K6, k2tog, k41, k2togtbl, k12, k2tog, k41, k2togtbl, k6. (102 sts)

Next round: K5, k2tog, k41, k2togtbl, k10, k2tog, k41, k2togtbl, k5. (98 sts)

Next round: K4, k2tog, k41, k2togtbl, k8, k2tog, k41, k2togtbl, k4. (94 sts)

Next round: K3, k2tog, k41, k2togtbl, k6, k2tog, k41, k2togtbl, k3. (90 sts)

Next round: K2, k2tog, k41, k2togtbl, k4, k2tog, k41, k2togtbl, k2. (86 sts)

Next round: K1, k2tog, k41, k2togtbl, k2, k2tog, k41, k2togtbl, k1. (82 sts)

Next round: K2tog, k41, k2togtbl, k2tog, k41, k2togtbl. (78 sts)

Follow Jazzy Bag pattern from **, pushing 39 sts along to each needle point, to
complete bag.

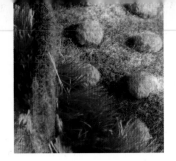

orange fluff and bobble

You will need

- 250g of Knitting4fun Natural Merino Wool in Grey (A)
- 50g of Ice Long Eyelash in Orange 8814 (B)
- 100g of Knitting4fun Pure Wool in Orange (C)
- 7mm (60cm/24 in. long) circular needle
- 10mm (80cm/32 in. long) circular needle
- Two 10mm double-pointed needles
- Knitter's sewing needle or bodkin for sewing
- Large snap fastener or press stud (optional)

Finished size

Bag measures approx 23cm/9 in. high by 25cm/10 in. wide.

Tension

12 stitches and 14 rows to 10cm/4 in. over st st on 10mm needles using two strands of A held together, although tension is not crucial in felting.

I am a little bobble crazy – I just adore them. The colours in this particular bag were inspired by a jacket I saw in a department store: I loved the grey and burnt orange colours together. This bag is one of many fluff and bobble bags I have made in just about every conceivable colour combination.

The Ice Long Eyelash yarn has, as the name suggests, long strands of eyelash and this gives a very thick and luxurious trim to the top of the bag.

I have also made the bag without the eyelash top and just knitted the first few rows at the top in moss stitch to stop the top edge from curling over. The i-cord handles can be made in a variety of lengths to suit your needs.

The three-needle cast off gives a very neat finish, so there is very little sewing up to be done. Once the bag is felted it appears seamless, giving a neat and professional look.

Abbreviations

MB = make bobble: with two strands of contrast colour (k1, p1, k1) into next st, turn p3, turn k3, turn p3, turn sk2po, slip the stitch back onto the left-hand needle and knit into it again using main colour; cut contrast yarn, pull ends of contrast yarn tight to form the bobble, knot ends together and sew them into the back of the bobble before felting. Alternatively, strand contrast colour on the wrong side between bobbles and cut yarn at the end of each bobble row.

For a smaller bobble, use one strand of colour and 7mm needle to knit the bobble and then return to 10mm needles when knitting the main colour.

See also page 125.

Bag

Using 7mm circular needle and one strand each of A and B held together, cast on 70 sts.

Join the cast on row into a circle, ensuring that the knitting is not twisted, and place a marker to establish the beginning of the round.

Purl 7 to 9 rounds, or until the trim at the top of the bag is the desired depth. Purling the stitches helps to keep the textured yarn on the right side of the knitting. Tease out the long fibres as you work so that they do not get trapped in the knitted fabric.*

Break off B and join in another strand of A.

Next round: [K6, inc] ten times. (80 sts)

Change to 10mm circular needle and cont in knit stitch.

Knit 5 rounds.

Round 6 (bobble round): [K7, MB] to the end of the row.

Knit 7 rounds.

Round 14 (bobble round): K4 [MB, k7] to last 4 sts, MB, k3.

Knit 7 rounds.

Round 22 (bobble round): As round 6.

Knit 7 rounds.

Round 30 (bobble round): As round 14.

Knit 7 rounds.

Round 38 (bobble round): As round 6.

Knit 7 rounds.

Round 46 (bobble round): As round 14.

Knit 5 rounds.

Shape base

Slip marker to the right-hand needle and start the shaping as folls:

Round 52: K5, k2tog, k26, k2togtbl, k10, k2tog, k26, k2togtbl, k5. (76 sts)

Round 53: K4, k2tog, k26, k2togtbl, k8, k2tog, k26, k2togtbl, k4. (72 sts)

Round 54: K3, k2tog, k26, k2togtbl, k6, k2tog, k26, k2togtbl, k3. (68 sts)

Round 55: K2, k2tog, k26, k2togtbl, k4, k2tog, k26, k2togtbl, k2. (64 sts)

Round 56: K1, k2tog, k26, k2togtbl, k2, k2tog, k26, k2togtbl, k1. (60 sts)

Round 57: K2tog, k26, k2togtbl, k2tog, k26, k2togtbl. (56 sts)

Join base

Turn the bag inside out and push 28 sts along to each needle point. Put both needle points together and, using another knitting needle (the same size as the circular needle or a size larger), knit tog the first st on each needle point. Knit tog the second st on each needle point, then slip the first st over the second st, so casting off (not too tightly) and joining the base of the bag at the same time. Rep until all sts are cast off.

Handle (make one)

Using 10mm double-pointed needles and two strands of A held together, cast on 4 sts.

Knit 1 row.

Switch needles in your hands, so the needle with the stitches on is in your left hand again. Slide the stitches to the other end of the needle and, pulling the yarn across the back of the stitches, knit the row again. The first three or four rows will be flat but don't worry, after that the knitting will become tubular. Before knitting the first stitch of each row, give the yarn a tug to make the strand across the back disappear.

Cont in this way, sliding and knitting, until the handle is the required length. As the handles will shrink by approximately one-third during felting, I usually knit about 50–60 rows for a short hand-held handle, 100 rows for a longer hand-held handle and 120–140 rows for a shoulder handle.

Cast off.

To make up

Using the knitter's sewing needle and A, sew the handle to the inside of the trim section at the top of the bag, about 1.5cm/½ in. down from the top edge.

Darn in all loose ends.

Following the instructions on pages 123–124, machine-wash the bag to felt it.

You can sew on a large snap fastener or press stud to fasten the bag if desired.

red fluff and bobble

This dramatic bag is knitted following the same pattern as Orange Fluff And Bobble, but using black wool for the main colour with red bobbles and top trim.

> This bag is one of many fluff and bobble bags I have made in just about every conceivable colour combo.

anything goes stash bag

You will need

- 200g of Knitting4fun Pure Merino Wool (A)
- Small amounts of eyelash, feather and other fancy yarns
- 8mm (40cm/16 in. or 60cm/24 in. long) circular needle
- 10mm (60cm/24 in. long) circular needle
- Knitter's sewing needle or bodkin for sewing
- Large snap fastener or press stud (optional)

Finished size

Bag measures approx 20cm/8 in. high by 20cm/8 in. wide.

Tension

12 stitches and 14 rows to 10cm/4 in. over st st on 10mm needles using two strands of A held together, although tension is not crucial in felting.

What do you do with all the bits of yarns that you have lying around? I had lots of eyelash yarns, feather yarns, ribbon yarns and other fancy types and just wanted to use up some of these small bits. This 'bitsa' bag was my answer; 'with bits of this and bits of that', it's a great stash buster. I have used Turquoise and Fuchsia Knitting4fun yarns as those colours worked perfectly with the fancy yarns I had.

The bag is knitted in pure wool and the other yarns are added in randomly throughout to create texture, using slip stitches, bobbles and other stitch patterns. Anything goes and your imagination is the only limit. You can achieve wonderful textures by just adding a fancy yarn to one strand of the wool and knitting them together. You do not have to knit a complete row in each chosen yarn – they can be very random.

The ends of the yarns can be left hanging out if you do not want to sew or weave them in. This gives great added texture, resembling tassels and fringes. An i-cord handle completes the bag, which can then be embellished further with textured yarns or with buttons and beads.

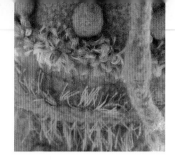

Abbreviations

MB = make bobble: with two strands of contrast colour (k1, p1, k1) into next st, turn p3, turn k3, turn p3, turn sk2po, slip the stitch back onto the left-hand needle and knit into it again using main colour; cut contrast yarn, pull ends of contrast yarn tight to form the bobble, knot ends together and sew them into the back of the bobble before felting. Alternatively, strand contrast colour on the wrong side between bobbles and cut yarn at the end of each bobble row.

For a smaller bobble, use one strand of colour and 8mm needle to knit the bobble and then return to 10mm needles when knitting the main colour.

See also page 125.

Bag

*Using 8mm circular needle and one strand each of A and fancy yarn held together, cast on 55 sts.

Join the cast on row into a circle, ensuring that the knitting is not twisted, and place a marker to establish the beginning of the round.

Purl 6 rounds, or until the trim at the top of the bag is the desired depth. Purling the stitches helps to keep the textured yarn on the right side of the knitting. Tease out the long fibres as you work so that they do not get trapped in the knitted fabric.

Break off the fancy yarn and join in another strand of A.

Round 7: [K11, M1] five times. (60 sts)

Change to 10mm circular needle and cont in knit stitch.

Knit 35 rounds using whatever patterning you choose.* Here are some ideas:

Textured yarns

If you are adding an eyelash or feather yarn, change to purl stitch to keep the textured yarn on the right side of the knitting.

Bobbles

Bobble round: [K5, MB in contrast colour] to the end of the row.

Slip stitch sequence

Knit two rows.

Round 3: [K5, sl1] to the end of the row.

Round 4: As round 3.

If you wish, you can now add a different slip stitch row and change colours.

Round 5: K2, sl1, [K5, sl1] to last 3 sts, k3.

Shape base

Slip marker to the right-hand needle and start the shaping as folls:

Round 43: K3, k2tog, k20, k2togtbl, k6, k2tog, k20, k2togtbl, k3. (56 sts)

Round 44: K2, k2tog, k20, k2togtbl, k4, k2tog, k20, k2togtbl, k2. (52 sts)

Round 45: K1, k2tog, k20, k2togtbl, k2, k2tog, k20, k2togtbl, k1. (48 sts)

Round 46: K2tog, k20, k2togtbl, k2tog, k20, k2togtbl. (44 sts)

Join base

Turn the bag inside out and push 22 sts along to each needle point. Put both needle points together and, using another knitting needle (the same size as the circular needle or a size larger), knit tog the first st on each needle point. Knit tog the second st on each needle point, then slip the first st over the second st, so casting off (not too tightly) and joining the base of the bag at the same time. Rep until all sts are cast off.

Handle (make one)

Using 10mm double-pointed needles and two strands of A held together, cast on 3 sts.

Knit 1 row.

Switch needles in your hands, so the needle with the stitches on is in your left hand again. Slide the stitches to the other end of the needle and, pulling the yarn across the back of the stitches, knit the row again. The first three or four rows will be flat but don't worry, after that the knitting will become tubular. Before knitting the first stitch of each row, give the yarn a tug to make the strand across the back disappear.

Cont in this way, sliding and knitting, until the handle is the required length. As the handles will shrink by approximately one-third during felting, I usually knit about 50–60 rows for a short hand-held handle, 100 rows for a longer hand-held handle and 120–140 rows for a shoulder handle.

Cast off.

You can work the handles in stripes, crochet a cord and twist it around the knitted cord (see page 21) or twist two or more crocheted or French-knitted cords together.

To make up

Using the knitter's sewing needle and A, sew the handle to the inside of the trim section at the top of the bag, about 1.5cm/½ in. down from the top edge.

Darn in all loose ends.

Following the instructions on pages 123–124, machine-wash the bag to felt it.

You can sew on a large snap fastener or press stud to fasten the bag if desired.

Anything goes and your imagination is the only limit. You can achieve wonderful textures by just adding a fancy yarn to one strand of the wool and knitting them together.

rounded stash bag

Work as for Anything Goes Stash Bag from * to *.

Shape base

Slip marker to the right-hand needle and start the shaping as folls:

Next round: [K8, k2tog] to the end of the round. (54 sts)

Knit 2 rounds.

Next round: [K7, k2tog] to the end of the round. (48 sts)

Knit 1 round.

Change to 10mm double-pointed needles as folls:

Next round: *[K6, k2tog] twice onto one double-pointed needle; rep from * onto two more needles. (42 sts)

Cont shaping on double-pointed needles as folls:

Knit 1 round.

Next round: [K5, k2tog] to the end of the round. (36 sts)

Next round: [K4, k2tog] to the end of the round. (30 sts)

Next round: [K3, k2tog] to the end of the round. (24 sts)

Next round: [K2, k2tog] to the end of the round. (18 sts)

Next round: [K1, k2tog] to the end of the round. (12 sts)

Next round: [K2tog] to the end of the round. (6 sts)

Leaving a 40cm/15 in. tail, cut yarn. Thread tail through rem sts. Thread tail into knitter's sewing needle and sew through these sts several times to secure the end.

Make handle and make up as for Anything Goes Stash Bag.

retro button bag

You will need

- 250g of Knitting4fun Pure Wool in Brown (A)
- 50g Katia Cancan in Brown (B)
- 8mm (60cm/24 in. long) circular needle
- 10mm (60cm/24 in. or 80cm/32 in. long) circular needle
- Two 10mm double-pointed needles
- Knitter's sewing needle or bodkin for sewing
- Buttons for decoration
- Sewing needle and thread
- Large snap fastener or press stud (optional)

Finished size

Bag measures approx 24cm/9½ in. high by 25cm/10 in. wide.

I have fond memories of sorting through my grandmother's button box and I eventually inherited some of the wonderful buttons. What do you do with all of these buttons, especially the precious ones with memories attached? It seems a shame to have them hidden away in tins, boxes and drawers. I decided to use them on my bags and I have decorated many bags with buttons old and new.

The buttons can be layered, which means that some of the less interesting ones can be stacked to give depth and add colour. So use up your button stash and enjoy them, after all you can always cut them off again and use them on something else when you have had enough of that particular bag.

I sew the buttons on after felting, as the first time I made one of these bags I planned the positions of the buttons, taking about three hours to sew them on, carefully spacing them and arranging the colours, forgetting that when the bag was felted the positions would move. I had to cut some buttons off and change the positions to get a better effect.

Tension

12 stitches and 14 rows to 10cm/4 in. over st st on 10mm needles using two strands of A held together, although tension is not crucial in felting.

Abbreviations

See page 125.

Bag

Using 8mm circular needle and one strand each of A and B held together, cast on 65 sts.

Join the cast on row into a circle, ensuring that the knitting is not twisted, and place a marker to establish the beginning of the round.

Purl 8 rounds, or until the trim at the top of the bag is the desired depth. Purling the stitches helps to keep the textured yarn on the right side of the knitting. Tease out the long fibres as you work so that they do not get trapped in the knitted fabric.

Break off B and join in another strand of A.

Round 9: [K12, inc] five times. (70 sts)

Change to 10mm circular needle and cont in knit stitch.

Knit 45 rounds using two strands of A held together.

Shape base

Slip marker to the right-hand needle and start the shaping as folls:

Round 55: K5, k2tog, k21, k2togtbl, k10, k2tog, k21, k2togtbl, k5. (66 sts)

Round 56: K4, k2tog, k21, k2togtbl, k8, k2tog, k21, k2togtbl, k4. (62 sts)

Round 57: K3, k2tog, k21, k2togtbl, k6, k2tog, k21, k2togtbl, k3. (58 sts)

Round 58: K2, k2tog, k21, k2togtbl, k4, k2tog, k21, k2togtbl, k2. (54 sts)

Round 59: K1, k2tog, k21, k2togtbl, k2, k2tog, k21, k2togtbl, k1. (50 sts)

Round 60: K2tog, k21, k2togtbl, k2tog, k21, k2togtbl. (46 sts)

Join base

Turn the bag inside out and push 23 sts along to each needle point. Put both needle points together and, using another knitting needle (the same size as the circular needle or a size larger), knit tog the first st on each needle point. Knit tog the second st on each needle point, then slip the first st over the second st, so casting off (not too tightly) and joining the base of the bag at the same time. Rep until all sts are cast off.

Handles (make two)

Using 10mm double-pointed needles and two strands of A held together, cast on 4 sts.

Knit 1 row.

Switch needles in your hands, so the needle with the stitches on is in your left hand again. Slide the stitches to the other end of the needle and, pulling the yarn across the back of the stitches, knit the row again. The first three or four rows will be flat but don't worry, after that the knitting will become tubular. Before knitting the first stitch of each row, give the yarn a tug to make the strand across the back disappear.

Cont in this way, sliding and knitting, until the handle is the required length. As the handles will shrink by approximately one-third during felting, I usually knit about 50–60 rows for a short hand-held handle, 100 rows for a longer hand-held handle and 120–140 rows for a shoulder handle.

Cast off.

To make up

Using the knitter's sewing needle and A, sew the handles to the inside of the trim section at the top of the bag, about 1.5cm/½ in. down from the top edge.

Darn in all loose ends.

Following the instructions on pages 123–124, machine-wash the bag to felt it.

Using the sewing needle and thread, sew the decorative buttons onto the felted bag. Stack two or three on top of one another or sew them on singly, as preferred.

You can sew on a large snap fastener or press stud to fasten the bag if desired.

What do you do with all your buttons, especially the precious ones with memories attached? It seems a shame to have them hidden away in tins, boxes and drawers.

slip stitch honeycomb

You will need

- 150g of Knitting4fun Pure Wool in Fuchsia (A)
- 50g of Ice Long Eyelash in each of Fuchsia 4112 and Orange 8814 (B and C)
- 150g of Knitting4fun Pure Wool in Orange (D)
- 8mm (60cm/24 in. long) circular needle
- 10mm (60cm/24 in. or 80cm/32 in. long) circular needle
- Pair of 8mm knitting needles
- Pair of plastic bag handles
- Knitter's sewing needle or bodkin for sewing
- Large snap fastener or press stud (optional)

Finished size

Bag measures approx 25cm/10 in. high by 27cm/10½ in. wide.

This bag was inspired by the outfit of a young Asian girl I met in Goa, India. The hot pink and orange colours of her sari just shone in the sunlight and I decided to make this bag in similar colours to keep that great memory alive.

The bag is knitted in a slip stitch design to create a honeycomb effect. I have used two different colours of Ice Long Eyelash yarn for the top edge so that I could mix pink and orange, giving a thick top with the two vivid colours shaded together.

The orange plastic handles complement the design and the colourway perfectly, though you could make i-cord handles if you prefer, like those on Pure Purple (see page 10).

This bag can be made in any colour combination to match any outfit. Alternatively, you can knit the honeycomb rows in a variety of different colours to create a stained-glass window effect.

Tension

12 stitches and 14 rows to 10cm/4 in. over st st on 10mm needles using two strands of A held together, although tension is not crucial in felting.

Abbreviations

See page 125.

Bag

Using 8mm circular needle and one strand each of A and B held together, cast on 80 sts.

Join the cast on row into a circle, ensuring that the knitting is not twisted, and place a marker to establish the beginning of the round.

Purl 8 rounds, using one strand each of A and C and one strand each of A and B on alternate rounds, or until the trim at the top of the bag is the desired depth. Purling the stitches helps to keep the textured yarn on the right side of the knitting. Tease out the long fibres as you work so that they do not get trapped in the knitted fabric.

Break off B and C and join in another strand of A.

Round 9: [K9, inc] eight times. (88 sts)

Change to 10mm circular needle.

Work honeycomb pattern using two strands of A or D (as appropriate) held together and stranding yarn not in use up the knitting on the wrong side.

Rounds 1–2: Knit in A.

Round 3: [Sl2, k6 in D] to the end of the row.

Rep round 3 five more times.

Rounds 9–10: Knit in A.

Round 11: K4 in D, [sl2, k6 in D] to last 4 sts, sl2, k2.

Rep round 11 five more times.

These 16 rounds form the pattern.

Rep the 16-round pattern three more times then rep rounds 1–10 once more.

Cut D and cont in 2 strands of A held together.

Shape base

Slip marker to the right-hand needle and start the shaping as folls:

Next round: K5, k2tog, k30, k2togtbl, k10, k2tog, k30, k2togtbl, k5. (84 sts)

Next round: K4, k2tog, k30, k2togtbl, k8, k2tog, k30, k2togtbl, k4. (80 sts)

Next round: K3, k2tog, k30, k2togtbl, k6, k2tog, k30, k2togtbl, k3. (76 sts)

Next round: K2, k2tog, k30, k2togtbl, k4, k2tog, k30, k2togtbl, k2. (72 sts)

Next round: K1, k2tog, k30, k2togtbl, k2, k2tog, k30, k2togtbl, k1. (68 sts)

Next round: K2tog, k30, k2togtbl, k2tog, k30, k2togtbl. (64 sts)

Join base

Turn the bag inside out and push 32 sts along to each needle point. Put both needle points together and, using another knitting needle (the same size as the circular needle or a size larger), knit tog the first st on each needle point. Knit tog the second st on each needle point, then slip the first st over the second st, so casting off (not too tightly) and joining the base of the bag at the same time. Rep until all sts are cast off.

Handle tabs (make four)

Using 8mm needles and one strand of A, cast on 4 sts.
  Knit 8 rows.
  Cast off.

To make up

Measure the space between the slots in the bag handles and mark the positions with pins on the inside of the top of the bag. Thread the knitter's sewing needle or bodkin with one strand of A and sew one narrow end of a strip to each marked point, about 1cm/¼ in. down from the top edge. Thread the strips through the slots in the plastic handles. Sew the other narrow end of each strip to the inside of the bag, about 1cm/¼ in. below the first end.

  Wrap the plastic handles tightly in bubble wrap and, with the bag right side out, fold the handles into the inside of the bag; this will protect them during the felting process in the washing machine. Close the bag opening with a safety pin or something similar to stop the handles from falling out.

  If you want to use a wooden, beaded or bamboo handle that cannot be put through the wash cycle, then sew one end of each strip in place as described. Felt the bag, then thread the felted strips through the slots and sew the free ends in place.

  Darn in all loose ends.

  Following the instructions on pages 123–124, machine-wash the bag to felt it.

  You can sew on a large snap fastener or press stud to fasten the bag if desired.

This bag was inspired by the outfit of a young Asian girl I met in Goa, India. The hot pink and orange colours of her sari just shone in the sunlight.

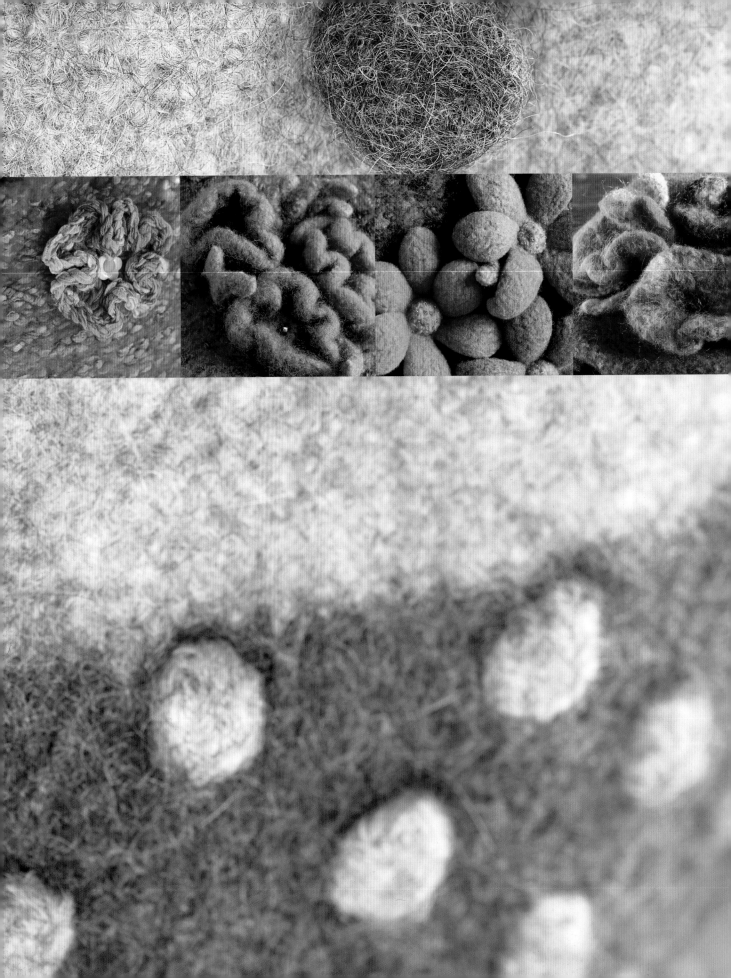

shaped
bags

With shaping at the top edge and around the base,
these bags are elegant, as well as useful, accessories.
Carry one on casual jeans days or smart suit days and
it'll look equally good.

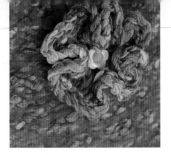

red wool and ribbon

You will need

- 100g of Knitting4fun Pure Wool in Red (A)
- 100g of Colinette Giotto in Fire 71 (B)
- 8mm (60cm/24 in. long) circular needle
- 10mm (60cm/24 in. long) circular needle
- Two 10mm double-pointed needles
- Pair of 8mm knitting needles
- Knitter's sewing needle or bodkin for sewing
- Decorative flower-shaped button
- Sewing needle and thread
- Large snap fastener or press stud (optional)

Finished size

Bag measures approx 18cm/7 in. high by 23cm/9 in. wide.

This dainty bag was made for a friend's teenage daughter who was going to a summer garden party. I chose the red wool colour to match the dress she was planning to wear.

The lovely variegated colours in the hand-dyed Colinette Giotto ribbon yarn are so exciting and they complement the red wool beautifully. When the bag is felted, the ribbon yarn produces a tweedy effect with a sheen that I just adore.

The ribbon flower is stitched to a brooch back so that it can be worn pinned to a dress or jacket, or just left on the bag. For a thoroughly co-ordinated look, make two flowers – one to embellish the bag and one to be worn as a corsage.

Tension

12 stitches and 14 rows to
10cm/4 in. over st st on
10mm needles using one
strand each of A and B held
together, although tension is
not crucial in felting.

Abbreviations

See page 125.

Bag

Using 8mm circular needle and one strand each of A and B held together, cast on 65 sts.

Join the cast on row into a circle, ensuring that the knitting is not twisted, and place a marker to establish the beginning of the round.

Round 1: [K1, p1] to last st, k1.

Round 2: [P1, k1] to last st, p1.

Rep rounds 1–2 once more then rep round 1 once more.

Round 6: [K12, inc] five times. (70 sts)

Change to 10mm circular needle and cont in knit stitch.

Knit 10 rounds.

Shape sides

Slip marker to the right-hand needle and start the shaping as folls:

Round 17: K3, M1, k29, M1, k6, M1, k29, M1, k3. (74 sts)

Knit 10 rounds.

Round 28: K4, M1, k29, M1, k8, M1, k29, M1, k4. (78 sts)

Knit 10 rounds.

Round 39: K5, M1, k29, M1, k10, M1, k29, M1, k5. (82 sts)

Knit 15 rounds.

Shape base

Slip marker to the right-hand needle and start the shaping as folls:

Round 55: K5, k2tog, k27, k2togtbl, k10, k2tog, k27, k2togtbl, k5. (78 sts)

Round 56: K4, k2tog, k27, k2togtbl, k8, k2tog, k27, k2togtbl, k4. (74 sts)

Round 57: K3, k2tog, k27, k2togtbl, k6, k2tog, k27, k2togtbl, k3. (70 sts)

Round 58: K2, k2tog, k27, k2togtbl, k4, k2tog, k27, k2togtbl, k2. (66 sts)

Round 59: K1, k2tog, k27, k2togtbl, k2, k2tog, k27, k2togtbl, k1. (62 sts)

Round 60: K2tog, k27, k2togtbl, k2tog, k27, k2togtbl. (58 sts)

Join base

Turn the bag inside out and push 29 sts along to each needle point. Put both needle points together and, using another knitting needle (the same size as the circular needle or a size larger), knit tog the first st on each needle point. Knit tog the second st on each needle point, then slip the first st over the second st, so casting off (not too tightly) and joining the base of the bag at the same time. Rep until all sts are cast off.

Flower

Using 8mm needles and one strand of B, cast on 63 sts.

Row 1 (RS): Knit.

Row 2: P1, p2tog, p1, p2togtbl, *p3, p2tog, p1, p2togtbl; rep from * to last st, p1. (47 sts)

Row 3: *Skpo, k1, k2tog, k1; rep from * to last 5 sts, skpo, k1, k2tog. (31 sts)

Row 4: P3tog *p1, p3tog; rep from * to the end of the row. (15 sts)

Row 5: Sk2po *k1, sk2po; rep from * to the end of the row. (7 sts)

Leaving a 40cm/15 in. tail, cut yarn. Thread tail through rem sts and pull up tightly. Thread tail into knitter's sewing needle and join seam to complete flower.

Handles (make two)

Using 10mm double-pointed needles and two strands of A held together, cast on 3 sts.

Knit 1 row.

Switch needles in your hands, so the needle with the stitches on is in your left hand again. Slide the stitches to the other end of the needle and, pulling the yarn across the back of the stitches, knit the row again. The first three or four rows will be flat but don't worry, after that the knitting will become tubular. Before knitting the first stitch of each row, give the yarn a tug to make the strand across the back disappear.

Cont in this way, sliding and knitting, until the handle is the required length. As the handles will shrink by approximately one-third during felting, I usually knit about 50–60 rows for a short hand-held handle, 100 rows for a longer hand-held handle and 120–140 rows for a shoulder handle.

Cast off.

To make up

Using the knitter's sewing needle and A, sew the handles to the inside of the trim section at the top of the bag, about 1.5cm/½ in. down from the top edge.

Using the knitter's sewing needle and A, sew the flower to the front of the bag.

Darn in all loose ends.

Following the instructions on pages 123–124, machine-wash the bag to felt it.

Using the sewing needle and thread, sew the button to the centre of the flower.

You can sew on a large snap fastener or press stud to fasten the bag if desired.

The lovely variegated colours in the hand-dyed Colinette Giotto ribbon yarn are so exciting and they complement the red wool beautifully.

cherry ripe

Having seen some beautiful, shiny cherries while visiting a market, I decided to make a cherry bag that was fun and funky. The cherries are knitted using red space-dyed yarn to give them a really ripe, fresh look. Each cherry is a small knitted bobble that is stuffed using some wool tops or some toy stuffing.

To give the leaves some shading they are knitted in green space-dyed yarn The subtly variegated colours of these space-dyed yarns work really well for knitting flowers, leaves and berries – anything natural in fact.

Once the leaves and cherries are complete, they are stitched together into a bunch and sewn onto the bag. If you love these perky fruit motifs, then you can knit more of them and make the Bunch of Cherries bag on page 64.

Finished size

Bag measures approx
23cm/9 in. high by
29cm/11½ in. wide.

Tension

12 stitches and 14 rows to
10cm/4 in. over st st on
10mm needles using one
strand each of A and B held
together, although tension is
not crucial in felting.

Abbreviations

See page 125.

Bag

Using 8mm circular needle and one strand each of A and B held together, cast on
75 sts.

Join the cast on row into a circle, ensuring that the knitting is not twisted, and
place a marker to establish the beginning of the round.

Round 1: [K1, p1] to last st, k1.

Round 2: [P1, k1] to last st, p1.

Rep rounds 1–2 twice more.

Round 7: [K14, inc] five times. (80 sts)

Change to 10mm circular needle and cont in knit stitch.

Knit 10 rounds.

Shape sides

Slip marker to the right-hand needle and start the shaping as folls:

Round 18: K4, M1, k32, M1, k8, M1, k32, M1, k4. (84 sts)

Knit 10 rounds.

Round 29: K5, M1, k32, M1, k10, M1, k32, M1, k5. (88 sts)

Knit 10 rounds.

Round 40: K6, M1, k32, M1, k12, M1, k32, M1, k6. (92 sts)

Knit 15 rounds.

Shape base

Slip marker to the right-hand needle and start the shaping as folls:

Round 56: K6, k2tog, k30, k2togtbl, k12, k2tog, k30, k2togtbl, k6. (88 sts)

Round 57: K5, k2tog, k30, k2togtbl, k10, k2tog, k30, k2togtbl, k5. (84 sts)

Round 58: K4, k2tog, k30, k2togtbl, k8, k2tog, k30, k2togtbl, k4. (80 sts)

Round 59: K3, k2tog, k30, k2togtbl, k6, k2tog, k30, k2togtbl, k3. (76 sts)

Round 60: K2, k2tog, k30, k2togtbl, k4, k2tog, k30, k2togtbl, k2. (72 sts)

Round 61: K1, k2tog, k30, k2togtbl, k2, k2tog, k30, k2togtbl, k1. (68 sts)

Round 62: K2tog, k30, k2togtbl, k2tog, k30, k2togtbl. (64 sts)

Join base

Turn the bag inside out and push 32 sts along to each needle point. Put both needle
points together and, using another knitting needle (the same size as the circular
needle or a size larger), knit tog the first st on each needle point. Knit tog the
second st on each needle point, then slip the first st over the second st, so casting
off (not too tightly) and joining the base of the bag at the same time. Rep until all sts
are cast off.

Handle tabs (make four)

Using 8mm needles and one strand of A, cast on 4 sts.
　Knit 8 rows.
　Cast off.

Cherry (make three)

Using 8mm needles and one strand of C, cast on 3 sts.
Row 1 (RS): Inc in each stitch. (6 sts)
　Starting with a purl row, work 5 rows st st.
Row 7: [K2tog] 3 times. (3 sts)
Row 8: Sl1, p2tog, psso.
　Leaving a 50cm/20 in. tail, cut yarn and fasten off.
　Thread knitter's sewing needle or bodkin with tail and sew side seam to form a large bobble, stuffing bobble lightly as you sew. Darn in the end.

Leaf (make three)

Using 8mm needles and one strand of D, cast on 3 sts.
Row 1 (RS): Knit.
Row 2 and all alt rows: Purl.
Row 3: K1, M1, k1, M1, k1. (5 sts)
Row 5: K1, M1, k3, M1, k1. (7 sts)
Rows 7 and 9: Knit.
Row 11: K1, k2tog, k1, k2tog, k1. (5 sts)
Row 13: K2tog, k1, k2tog. (3 sts)
Row 14: Sl1, p2tog, psso.
　Leaving a 50cm/20 in. tail, cut yarn and fasten off.

To make up

　Using tails of yarn, the knitter's sewing needle or bodkin and following photograph for position, sew leaves in a group to front of bag.
　Thread a double strand of D through the top of each cherry and sew them on to the bag below the leaves, leaving about 8cm/3 in. of green yarn free above the cherry for the stalk. The strands will join together during the felting process to make a single, slim stalk. Alternatively, join D to the cherry and crochet a 8cm/3 in. chain before sewing the cherry to the bag.

The subtly variegated colours of these space-dyed yarns work really well for knitting flowers, leaves and berries.

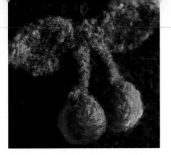

Measure the space between the slots in the bag handles and mark the positions with pins on the inside of the top of the bag. Thread the knitter's sewing needle or bodkin with one strand of A and sew one narrow end of a strip to each marked point, about 1cm/¼ in. down from the top edge. Thread the strips through the slots in the plastic handles. Sew the other narrow end of each strip to the inside of the bag, about 1cm/¼ in. below the first end.

Wrap the plastic handles tightly in bubble wrap and, with the bag right side out, fold the handles into the inside of the bag; this will protect them during the felting process in the washing machine. Close the bag opening with a safety pin or something similar to stop the handles from falling out.

If you want to use a wooden, beaded or bamboo handle that cannot be put through the wash cycle, then sew one end of each strip in place as described. Felt the bag, then thread the felted strips through the slots and sew the free ends in place.

Darn in all loose ends.

Following the instructions on pages 123–124, machine-wash the bag to felt it.

You can sew on a large snap fastener or press stud to fasten the bag if desired.

bunch of cherries

This bag is made following the same pattern as Cherry Ripe, but using two strands of Knitting4fun Pure Wool in Black. Twelve cherries and twelve leaves are made and sewn in groups of two around the top edge (front and back) of the bag.

recycled sari silk bag

I have collected many different skeins of recycled sari silk yarns in wonderful jewel-like colours, but what do you do with all of them? I keep them in glass vases just to look at, but I did want to try to use some of them in a bag.

For this design I knitted one strand of pure wool and one strand of the sari silk yarn together. As the sari silk is hand-spun and every skein is different, I had to knit from two balls at the same time, alternating them on each row so that the colours blended well. Once felted, the sari silk is trapped by the wool, leaving a textured surface with lots of jewel colours popping through the main colour.

I made different flowers to decorate the bag – larger ones, clusters of small ones and leaves or corkscrew leaf tendrils. I sewed some to brooch backs, so that they can be removed and the decorations can be changed.

In Nepal I found some banana fibre yarn with similar random colours, but a little more sheen than the sari silk yarn. I made the purple bag on page 70 from this yarn – it doesn't smell of bananas though!

Tension

12 stitches and 14 rows to 10cm/4 in. over st st on 10mm needles using one strand each of A and B held together, although tension is not crucial in felting.

Abbreviations

See page 125.

Bag

Using 8mm circular needle and one strand each of A and B held together, cast on 75 sts.

Join the cast on row into a circle, ensuring that the knitting is not twisted, and place a marker to establish the beginning of the round.

Round 1: [K1, p1] to last st, k1.

Round 2: [P1, k1] to last st, p1.

Rep rounds 1–2 twice more.

Round 7: [K14, inc] five times. (80 sts)

Change to 10mm circular needle and cont in knit stitch.

Knit 10 rounds.

Shape sides

Slip marker to the right-hand needle and start the shaping as folls:

Round 18: K4, M1, k32, M1, k8, M1, k32, M1, k4. (84 sts)

Knit 10 rounds.

Round 29: K5, M1, k32, M1, k10, M1, k32, M1, k5. (88 sts)

Knit 10 rounds.

Round 40: K6, M1, k32, M1, k12, M1, k32, M1, k6. (92 sts)

Knit 15 rounds.

Shape base

Slip marker to the right-hand needle and start the shaping as folls:

Round 56: K6, k2tog, k30, k2togtbl, k12, k2tog, k30, k2togtbl, k6. (88 sts)

Round 57: K5, k2tog, k30, k2togtbl, k10, k2tog, k30, k2togtbl, k5. (84 sts)

Round 58: K4, k2tog, k30, k2togtbl, k8, k2tog, k30, k2togtbl, k4. (80 sts)

Round 59: K3, k2tog, k30, k2togtbl, k6, k2tog, k30, k2togtbl, k3. (76 sts)

Round 60: K2, k2tog, k30, k2togtbl, k4, k2tog, k30, k2togtbl, k2. (72 sts)

Round 61: K1, k2tog, k30, k2togtbl, k2, k2tog, k30, k2togtbl, k1. (68 sts)

Round 62: K2tog, k30, k2togtbl, k2tog, k30, k2togtbl. (64 sts)

Join base

Turn the bag inside out and push 32 sts along to each needle point. Put both needle points together and, using a knitting needle (the same size as the circular needle or a size larger), knit tog the first st on each needle point. Knit tog the second st on each needle point, then slip the first st over the second st, so casting off (not too tightly) and joining the base of the bag at the same time. Rep until all sts are cast off.

Handle tabs (make four)

Using 8mm needles and one strand of A, cast on 4 sts.

Knit 8 rows.

Cast off.

Flower

Using 8mm needles and one strand of wool or mohair, cast on 63 sts.

Work flower in coloured stripes for best effect.

Row 1: Knit.

Row 2: P1, p2tog, p1, p2togtbl, *p3, p2tog, p1, p2togtbl; rep from * to last st, p1. (47 sts)

Row 3: *Skpo, k1, k2tog, k1; rep from * to last 5 sts, skpo, k1, k2tog. (31 sts)

Row 4: P3tog, *p1, p3tog; rep from * to the end of the row. (15 sts)

Row 5: Sk2po, *k1, sk2po; rep from * to the end of the row. (7 sts)

Leaving a 40cm/15 in. tail, cut yarn. Thread tail through rem sts and pull up tightly. Thread tail into knitter's sewing needle and join seam to complete flower.

Leaf cluster

Using one strand of pure wool or mohair and 8mm knitting needles, cast on 15 sts.

Row 1: *Cast off 14 sts, slip rem st onto the left-hand needle, cast on 14 sts; *rep from * two or three more times. Leaving a 50cm/20 in. tail, cut yarn and fasten off.

To make up

Using tails of yarn and following the photograph for position, sew flowers and leaves in a group to the front of the bag. You can sew a decorative bead into the centre of each flower.

Measure the space between the slots in the bag handles and mark the positions with pins on the inside of the top of the bag. Thread the knitter's sewing needle or bodkin with one strand of A and sew one narrow end of a strip to each marked point, about 1cm/¼ in. down from the top edge. Thread the strips through the slots in the plastic handles. Sew the other narrow end of each strip to the inside of the bag, about 1cm/¼ in. below the first end.

Wrap the plastic handles tightly in bubble wrap and, with the bag right side out, fold the handles into the inside of the bag; this will protect them during the felting process in the washing machine. Close the bag opening with a safety pin or something similar to stop the handles from falling out.

If you want to use a wooden, beaded or bamboo handle that cannot be put through the wash cycle, then sew one end of each strip in place as described. Felt the bag, then thread the felted strips through the slots and sew the free ends in place.

Darn in all loose ends.

Following the instructions on pages 123–124, machine-wash the bag to felt it.

You can sew on a large snap fastener or press stud to fasten the bag if desired.

Once felted, the sari silk is trapped by the wool, leaving a textured surface with lots of jewel colours popping through the main colour.

banana fibre bag

Swap the recycled sari yarn for banana fibre then follow the same pattern to make this bag. The flower and leaves are made using the following patterns.

You will need
- 125g of Knitting4fun Pure Wool in Violet (A)
- 400g of Knitting4fun Banana Fibre Kaleidoscope Yarn (B)

Large flower
Using one strand of pure wool and 8mm knitting needles, cast on 15 sts.
Row 1: K14, turn.
Row 2: Sl1, k12, turn.
Row 3: Sl1, k11, turn.
Row 4: Sl1, k10, turn.
Cont as set, slipping 1 st and knitting 9, 8, 7, 6, 5, 4, 3 sts on consecutive rows.
Row 12: Sl1, knit to the end of the row.
Row 13: Skpo, then cast off all sts.
   Leave rem st on needle and cast on 10 more sts. (11 sts)
   Rep rows 1–13 four or five times more to give five or six petals, as desired.
   Leaving a 50cm/20 in. tail, cut yarn. Thread knitter's sewing needle or bodkin with tail and sew through the edge of each petal and gather up, pulling the petals into a ring. Sew through the centre to hold the flower together. This pattern makes the pink flower shown opposite. To make the smaller flowers shown above left, cast on 11 sts and follow the large flower pattern on page 99.

Flower centre
Using 8mm needles and one strand of pure fine wool, cast on 3 sts.
Row 1 (RS): Inc in each stitch. (6 sts)
   Starting with a purl row, work 5 rows st st.
Row 7: [K2tog] 3 times. (3 sts)
Row 8: Sl1, p2tog, psso.
   Leaving a 50cm/20 in. tail, cut yarn and fasten off.
   Thread knitter's sewing needle or bodkin with tail and sew side seam to form a large bobble, stuffing bobble lightly as you sew. Darn in the end.

Corkscrew leaf
Using 8mm knitting needles and one strand of fine pure wool, cast on 40 sts.
Row 1: [K2tog] to the end of the row. (20 sts)
Row 2: [K2tog] to the end of the row. (10 sts)
   Cast off.
   Make 2 or 3 leaves; you can vary the size by casting on more or fewer stitches.
   Using the tails of yarn and following the photograph for position, sew the leaves to the bag. Sew the flower centre into the petals and sew the flower to the bag.

little saddle bag

You will need

- 200g of Knitting4fun Pure Wool in Deep Pink (A)
- 200g of Lang Mille Colori in colour 65 (B)
- 8mm (80cm/32 in. long) circular needle
- 10mm (80cm/32 in. long) circular needle
- Pair of 8mm knitting needles
- Pair of 10mm knitting needles
- Knitter's sewing needle or bodkin for sewing
- Button or toggle for fastening

Finished size

Bag measures approx 19cm/7½ in. high by 22cm/8½ in. wide.

I found myself having to use crutches for a while and suddenly realised how hard it is to carry things while using crutches. I had always made my bags with shorter handles, but now I needed a bag that I could wear across my body, leaving my hands free.

I made this bag from a pure wool yarn and a random-dyed yarn that is 50 per cent super-wash wool and 50 per cent acrylic, which when felted gives a lovely bouclé effect.

I used moss stitch for the strap so that it stayed flat and was comfortable to wear. As my hands were occupied (by the crutches) I also needed extra security, so this bag has a flap with a button closure. The button was stitched on with the pure wool so that it felted into position, making it a strong fastening.

This style of bag can be made in any size: larger sizes are great for laptops and smaller sizes are ideal for carrying bottles of water – you can't carry mugs of tea when you are on crutches!

Tension

12 stitches and 14 rows to 10cm/4 in. over st st on 10mm needles using one strand each of A and B held together, although tension is not crucial in felting.

Abbreviations

See page 125.

Bag

Using 8mm circular needle and one strand each of A and B held together, cast on 75 sts.

Join the cast on row into a circle, ensuring that the knitting is not twisted, and place a marker to establish the beginning of the round.

Round 1: [K1, p1] to last st, k1.

Round 2: [P1, k1] to last st, p1.

Rep rounds 1–2 twice more.

Round 7: [K14, inc] five times. (80 sts)

Change to 10mm circular needle and cont in knit stitch.

Knit 10 rounds.

Shape sides

Slip marker to the right-hand needle and start the shaping as folls:

Round 18: K4, M1, k32, M1, k8, M1, k32, M1, k4. (84 sts)

Knit 10 rounds.

Round 29: K5, M1, k32, M1, k10, M1, k32, M1, k5. (88 sts)

Knit 10 rounds.

Round 40: K6, M1, k32, M1, k12, M1, k32, M1, k6. (92 sts)

Knit 5 rounds.

Shape base

Slip marker to the right-hand needle and start the shaping as folls:

Round 66: K6, k2tog, k30, k2togtbl, k12, k2tog, k30, k2togtbl, k6. (88 sts)

Round 67: K5, k2tog, k30, k2togtbl, k10, k2tog, k30, k2togtbl, k5. (84 sts)

Round 68: K4, k2tog, k30, k2togtbl, k8, k2tog, k30, k2togtbl, k4. (80 sts)

Round 69: K3, k2tog, k30, k2togtbl, k6, k2tog, k30, k2togtbl, k3. (76 sts)

Round 70: K2, k2tog, k30, k2togtbl, k4, k2tog, k30, k2togtbl, k2. (72 sts)

Round 71: K1, k2tog, k30, k2togtbl, k2, k2tog, k30, k2togtbl, k1. (68 sts)

Round 72: K2tog, k30, k2togtbl, k2tog, k30, k2togtbl. (64 sts)

Join base

Turn the bag inside out and push 32 sts along to each needle point. Put both needle points together and, using another knitting needle (the same size as the circular needle or a size larger), knit tog the first st on each needle point. Knit tog the second st on each needle point, then slip the first st over the second st, so casting off (not too tightly) and joining the base of the bag at the same time. Rep until all sts are cast off.

Flap

Lay the bag flat with the cast-off seam running along the bottom. In line with the first increase made in round 18, place a pin in the top edge of the back of the bag. On the same edge, place a second pin in line with the second increase.

With the right side facing, one strand each of A and B held together and 8mm knitting needles, pick up 33 sts between the pins.

Row 1: [K1, p1] to last st, k1.

Row 2: As row 1.

Change to 10mm knitting needles.

Rep row 1 ten more times.

Row 13: Inc, [p1, k1] to last 2 sts, p1, inc. (35 sts)

Row 14: [P1, k1] to last st, p1.

Rep row 14 nine more times.

Row 24: Inc [k1, p1] to last 2 sts, k1, inc. (37 sts)

Row 25: [K1, p1] to last st, k1.

Rep row 25 nine more times.

Row 35: K2togtbl, [k1, p1] to last 2 sts, k2tog. (35 sts)

Keeping moss st patt correct, rep row 35 four more times. (27 sts)

Row 40 (1st buttonhole row): K2togtbl, moss 10, cast off 3 sts, moss to last 2 sts, k2tog.

Row 41 (2nd buttonhole row): Moss 11, cast on 3 sts, moss 11. (25 sts)

Row 42: K2togtbl, moss to last 2 sts, k2tog. (23 sts)

Keeping moss st patt correct, rep row 42 three more times. (17 sts)

Cast off.

Handle

Using 8mm knitting needles and one strand of A, pick up 5 sts along the top edge of the bag at one side of the flap.

Row 1: K1, p1, k1, p1, k1.

Rep row 1 until handle measures 120cm/48 in. long.

Cast off.

To make up

Using the knitter's sewing needle and A, sew the free end of the handle to the opposite top edge of the bag.

Darn in all loose ends.

Following the instructions on pages 123–124, machine-wash the bag to felt it.

Sew the toggle to the front of the bag to align with the buttonhole in the flap.

I made this bag from a pure wool yarn and a random-dyed yarn that is 50 per cent super-wash wool and 50 per cent acrylic, which when felted gives a lovely bouclé effect.

acorn and oak leaf

You will need

- 150g of Knitting4fun Pure Wool in Apple Green (A)
- 125g of Noro Kureyon in 201 (B)
- Small amounts of Knitting4fun Pure Wool in Gold (C) and Brown (D)
- Small amount of Knitting4fun Space-dyed Pure Wool in Green (E)
- 8mm (60cm/24 in. long) circular needle
- 10mm (80cm/32 in. long) circular needle
- Pair of 8mm knitting needles
- Pair of plastic bag handles
- Knitter's sewing needle or bodkin for sewing
- Small amount of stuffing
- Large snap fastener or press stud (optional)

Finished size

Bag measures approx 24cm/9½ in. high by 29cm/11½ in. wide.

This is my Sherwood Forest bag. I live in Nottingham, England, the home of Robin Hood, where legend has it that Robin lived with his band of outlaws among the mighty oaks in the depths of Sherwood Forest. There are many films that tell the story. (The idea of men in tights is still something I find a little worrying!)

This bag is knitted with Noro Kureyon yarn and a pure wool yarn held together to give the variegated colours of the forest in the autumn. Using small amounts of gold and brown pure wool for the acorns and space-dyed green pure wool for the leaves gives them a suitably naturalistic look.

The oak leaves and acorns that decorate the bag can be stitched on or they can be sewn to a brooch back so that they can be removed. A dark brown plastic handle completes the design.

Tension

12 stitches and 14 rows to 10cm/4 in. over st st on 10mm needles using one strand each of A and B held together, although tension is not crucial in felting.

Abbreviations

See page 125.

Bag

Using 8mm circular needle and one strand each of A and B held together, cast on 75 sts.

Join the cast on row into a circle, ensuring that the knitting is not twisted, and place a marker to establish the beginning of the round.

Round 1: [K1, p1] to last st, k1.

Round 2: [P1, k1] to last st, p1.

Rep rounds 1–2 twice more.

Round 7: [K14, inc] five times. (80 sts)

Change to 10mm circular needle and cont in knit stitch.

Knit 10 rounds.

Shape sides

Slip marker to the right-hand needle and start the shaping as folls:

Round 18: K4, M1, k32, M1, k8, M1, k32, M1, k4. (84 sts)

Knit 10 rounds.

Round 29: K5, M1, k32, M1, k10, M1, k32, M1, k5. (88 sts)

Knit 10 rounds.

Round 40: K6, M1, k32, M1, k12, M1, k32, M1, k6. (92 sts)

Knit 15 rounds.

Shape base

Slip marker to the right-hand needle and start the shaping as folls:

Round 56: K6, k2tog, k30, k2togtbl, k12, k2tog, k30, k2togtbl, k6. (88 sts)

Round 57: K5, k2tog, k30, k2togtbl, k10, k2tog, k30, k2togtbl, k5. (84 sts)

Round 58: K4, k2tog, k30, k2togtbl, k8, k2tog, k30, k2togtbl, k4. (80 sts)

Round 59: K3, k2tog, k30, k2togtbl, k6, k2tog, k30, k2togtbl, k3. (76 sts)

Round 60: K2, k2tog, k30, k2togtbl, k4, k2tog, k30, k2togtbl, k2. (72 sts)

Round 61: K1, k2tog, k30, k2togtbl, k2, k2tog, k30, k2togtbl, k1. (68 sts)

Round 62: K2tog, k30, k2togtbl, k2tog, k30, k2togtbl. (64 sts)

Join base

Turn the bag inside out and push 32 sts along to each needle point. Put both needle points together and, using another knitting needle (the same size as the circular needle or a size larger), knit tog the first st on each needle point. Knit tog the second st on each needle point, then slip the first st over the second st, so casting off (not too tightly) and joining the base of the bag at the same time. Rep until all sts are cast off.

Handle tabs (make four)

Using 8mm needles and one strand of A, cast on 4 sts.

Knit 8 rows.

Cast off.

Acorn (make 3)

Using 8mm needles and one strand of C, cast on 3 sts.

Row 1 (RS): Inc in each stitch. (6 sts)

Starting with a purl row, work 7 rows st st.

Row 7: [K2tog] three times. (3 sts)

Leaving a 50cm/20 in. tail, cut yarn and thread through rem sts.

Thread knitter's sewing needle or bodkin with tail and sew side seam to form a large bobble, stuffing bobble lightly as you sew. Darn in the end.

Acorn cup (make 3)

Using 8mm needles and one strand of D, cast on 8 sts.

Knit 4 rows.

Row 5: [K2tog] four times. (4 sts)

Leaving a 50cm/20 in. tail, cut yarn and thread through rem sts.

Thread knitter's sewing needle or bodkin with tail and sew side seam to form a cup. Sew the acorn into the cup.

Leaf (make three)

Using 8mm needles and one strand of E, make a slip knot 50cm/20 in. from end of yarn and cast on 3 sts.

Knit 2 rows.

Row 3: K1, M1, k1, M1, k1. (5 sts)

Row 4 and foll 2 alt rows: Knit.

Row 5: K2, M1, k1, M1, k2. (7 sts)

Row 7: K1, M1, k2, M1, k1, M1, k2, M1, k1. (11 sts)

Row 9: K2, M1, k7, M1, k2. (13 sts)

Row 10: Cast off 3 sts, knit to the end of the row. (10 sts)

Row 11: Cast off 3 sts, knit to the end of the row. (7 sts)

Row 12: Knit.

Rep rows 7–12 twice more.

This bag is knitted with Noro Kureyon yarn and a pure wool yarn held together to give the variegated colours of the forest in the autumn.

Row 25: Knit.
Row 26: K2togtbl, k3, k2tog. (5 sts)
Row 27: K2togtbl, k1, k2tog. (3 sts)
Row 28: Sk2po.

Cut yarn and fasten off. Darn in end.

To make up

Using tails of yarn and following the photograph for position, sew leaves in a group to front of bag.

Thread a double strand of D through the top of each acorn and sew them below the leaves, leaving about 6cm/2½ in. of brown yarn free above the acorn for the stalk. Alternatively, join D to the acorn and crochet a 6cm/2½ in. chain before sewing the acorn to the bag.

Measure the space between the slots in the bag handles and mark the positions with pins on the inside of the top of the bag. Thread the knitter's sewing needle or bodkin with one strand of A and sew one narrow end of a strip to each marked point, about 1cm/¼ in. down from the top edge. Thread the strips through the slots in the plastic handles. Sew the other narrow end of each strip to the inside of the bag, about 1cm/¼ in. below the first end.

Wrap the plastic handles tightly in bubble wrap and, with the bag right side out, fold the handles into the inside of the bag; this will protect them during the felting process in the washing machine. Close the bag opening with a safety pin or something similar to stop the handles from falling out.

If you want to use a wooden, beaded or bamboo handle that cannot be put through the wash cycle, then sew one end of each strip in place as described. Felt the bag, then thread the felted strips through the slots and sew the free ends in place.

Darn in all loose ends.

Following the instructions on pages 123–124, machine-wash the bag to felt it.

You can sew on a large snap fastener or press stud to fasten the bag if desired.

monochrome jazz

You will need

- 250g of Knitting4fun Pure Wool in Black (A)
- 50g of Elle Pizzazz in Zest 250 (B)
- 50g of Ice Long Eyelash in Black 7711 (C)
- 8mm (40cm/16 in. or 60cm/24 in. long) circular needle
- 10mm (60cm/24 in. or 80cm/32 in. long) circular needle
- Pair of 8mm knitting needles
- Pair of plastic bag handles
- Knitter's sewing needle or bodkin for sewing
- Large snap fastener or press stud (optional)

Finished size

Bag measures approx 24cm/9½ in. high by 29cm/11½ in. wide.

Being a colour fiend, black and white is an unusual combination for me, but it is very striking. I made this bag when I had an important business meeting to go to. As I had to wear a suit, I wanted my bag to be extra-funky so that I didn't look too formal.

The Elle Pizzazz yarn comes in a black and white colourway, so it was perfect for what I wanted. I added in a black eyelash yarn, too, and knitted the two fancy yarns together with the black wool yarn to make a wonderful textured trim for this stylish bag.

The black and white plastic handles do look good, but the bag also looks great with plain black handles or knitted i-cord ones.

Tension

12 stitches and 14 rows to 10cm/4 in. over st st on 10mm needles using two strands of A held together, although tension is not crucial in felting.

Abbreviations

See page 125.

Bag

Using 8mm circular needle and one strand each of A, B and C held together, cast on 75 sts.

Join the cast on row into a circle, ensuring that the knitting is not twisted, and place a marker to establish the beginning of the round.

Purl 8 rounds, or until the trim at the top of the bag is the desired depth. Purling the stitches helps to keep the textured yarn on the right side of the knitting. Tease out the long fibres as you work so that they do not get trapped in the knitted fabric.

Cut B and C and join in another strand of A.

Round 9: [K14, inc] five times. (80 sts)

Change to 10mm circular needle.

Knit 10 rounds.

Shape sides

Slip marker to the right-hand needle and start the shaping as folls:

Round 20: K4, M1, k32, M1, k8, M1, k32, M1, k4. (84 sts)

Knit 10 rounds.

Round 31: K5, M1, k32, M1, k10, M1, k32, M1, k5. (88 sts)

Knit 10 rounds.

Round 42: K6, M1, k32, M1, k12, M1, k32, M1, k6. (92 sts)

Knit 15 rounds.

Shape base

Slip marker to the right-hand needle and start the shaping as folls:

Round 58: K6, k2tog, k30, k2togtbl, k12, k2tog, k30, k2togtbl, k6. (88 sts)

Round 59: K5, k2tog, k30, k2togtbl, k10, k2tog, k30, k2togtbl, k5. (84 sts)

Round 60: K4, k2tog, k30, k2togtbl, k8, k2tog, k30, k2togtbl, k4. (80 sts)

Round 61: K3, k2tog, k30, k2togtbl, k6, k2tog, k30, k2togtbl, k3. (76 sts)

Round 62: K2, k2tog, k30, k2togtbl, k4, k2tog, k30, k2togtbl, k2. (72 sts)

Round 63: K1, k2tog, k30, k2togtbl, k2, k2tog, k30, k2togtbl, k1. (68 sts)

Round 64: K2tog, k30, k2togtbl, k2tog, k30, k2togtbl. (64 sts)

Join base

Turn the bag inside out and push 32 sts along to each needle point. Put both needle points together and, using another knitting needle (the same size as the circular needle or a size larger), knit tog the first st on each needle point. Knit tog the second st on each needle point, then slip the first st over the second st, so casting off (not too tightly) and joining the base of the bag at the same time. Rep until all sts are cast off.

Handle tabs (make four)

Using 8mm needles and one strand of A, cast on 4 sts.
   Knit 10 rows.
   Cast off.

To make up

Measure the space between the slots in the bag handles and mark the positions with pins on the inside of the top of the bag. Thread the knitter's sewing needle or bodkin with one strand of A and sew one narrow end of a strip to each marked point, about 1cm/¼ in. down from the top edge. Thread the strips through the slots in the plastic handles. Sew the other narrow end of each strip to the inside of the bag, about 1cm/¼ in. below the first end.

   Wrap the plastic handles tightly in bubble wrap and, with the bag right side out, fold the handles into the inside of the bag; this will protect them during the felting process in the washing machine. Close the bag opening with a safety pin or something similar to stop the handles from falling out.

   If you want to use a wooden, beaded or bamboo handle that cannot be put through the wash cycle, then sew one end of each strip in place as described. Felt the bag, then thread the felted strips through the slots and sew the free ends in place.

   Darn in all loose ends.

   Following the instructions on pages 123–124, machine-wash the bag to felt it.

   You can sew on a large snap fastener or press stud to fasten the bag if desired.

I made this bag when I had an important business meeting to go to. As I had to wear a suit, I wanted my bag to be extra-funky so that I didn't look too formal.

variegated stripe bag

You will need

- 100g of Knitting4fun Pure Wool in Jade Blue (A)
- 100g of Noro Kureyon in 173 (B)
- Small amounts of pure wool or mohair for flowers and leaves
- 8mm (40cm/16 in. or 60cm/24 in. long) circular needle
- 10mm (80cm/32 in. long) circular needle
- Pair of 8mm knitting needles
- Pair of plastic bag handles
- Knitter's sewing needle or bodkin for sewing
- Large snap fastener or press stud (optional)
- Decorative beads (optional)

Finished size

Bag measures approx 23cm/9 in. high by 29cm/11½ in. wide.

This has to be one of my favourite bags and is inspired by the wonderful colours available in the Japanese Noro Kureyon yarn. I have knitted so many bags using almost every shade of this yarn.

The Noro Kureyon yarn knits up to give a striped effect, so for this bag I blended it with one strand of pure wool yarn to get a more subtle variegated effect. The mix of yarns also gives a firmer felt than the Noro yarn gives when used alone.

These bags can be decorated with flowers – large ones, small ones, or clusters of either or both. Alternatively they can have no extra decoration at all; just enjoy the gorgeous colours of the blended yarns.

Using different-coloured plastic handles to complement the yarns, I have managed to achieve some wonderful results and now have bright, exciting bags to match every outfit.

Tension

12 stitches and 14 rows to 10cm/4 in. over st st on 10mm needles using one strand each of A and B held together, although tension is not crucial in felting.

Abbreviations

See page 125.

Bag

Using 8mm circular needle and one strand each of A and B held together, cast on 75 sts.

Join the cast on row into a circle, ensuring that the knitting is not twisted, and place a marker to establish the beginning of the round.

Round 1: [K1, p1] to last st, k1.

Round 2: [P1, k1] to last st, p1.

Rep rounds 1–2 twice more.

Round 7: [K14, inc] five times. (80 sts)

Change to 10mm circular needle and cont in knit stitch.

Knit 10 rounds.

Shape sides

Slip marker to the right-hand needle and start the shaping as folls:

Round 18: K4, M1, k32, M1, k8, M1, k32, M1, k4. (84 sts)

Knit 10 rounds.

Round 29: K5, M1, k32, M1, k10, M1, k32, M1, k5. (88 sts)

Knit 10 rounds.

Round 40: K6, M1, k32, M1, k12, M1, k32, M1, k6. (92 sts)

Knit 15 rounds.

Shape base

Slip marker to the right-hand needle and start the shaping as folls:

Round 56: K6, k2tog, k30, k2togtbl, k12, k2tog, k30, k2togtbl, k6. (88 sts)

Round 57: K5, k2tog, k30, k2togtbl, k10, k2tog, k30, k2togtbl, k5. (84 sts)

Round 58: K4, k2tog, k30, k2togtbl, k8, k2tog, k30, k2togtbl, k4. (80 sts)

Round 59: K3, k2tog, k30, k2togtbl, k6, k2tog, k30, k2togtbl, k3. (76 sts)

Round 60: K2, k2tog, k30, k2togtbl, k4, k2tog, k30, k2togtbl, k2. (72 sts)

Round 61: K1, k2tog, k30, k2togtbl, k2, k2tog, k30, k2togtbl, k1. (68 sts)

Round 62: K2tog, k30, k2togtbl, k2tog, k30, k2togtbl. (64 sts)

Join base

Turn the bag inside out and push 32 sts along to each needle point. Put both needle points together and, using another knitting needle (the same size as the circular needle or a size larger), knit tog the first st on each needle point. Knit tog the second st on each needle point, then slip the first st over the second st, so casting off (not too tightly) and joining the base of the bag at the same time. Rep until all sts are cast off.

Handle tabs (make four)

Using 8mm needles and one strand of A, cast on 4 sts.

Knit 10 rows.

Cast off.

Large flower

Using 8mm needles and one strand of wool or mohair, cast on 95 sts.

Work flower in coloured stripes for best effect.

Row 1: Knit.

Row 2: P1, p2tog, p1, p2togtbl, *p3, p2tog, p1, p2togtbl; rep from * to last st, p1. (71 sts)

Row 3: *Skpo, k1, k2tog, k1; rep from * to last 5 sts, skpo, k1, k2tog. (47 sts)

Row 4: P3tog, *p1, p3tog; rep from * to the end of the row. (23 sts)

Row 5: Sk2po, *k1, sk2po; rep from * to the end of the row. (11 sts)

Beginning with a purl row, work 2 rows st st.

Leaving a 40cm/15 in. tail, cut yarn. Thread tail through rem sts and pull up tightly.

Thread tail into knitter's sewing needle and join seam to complete flower.

Small flower

Using 8mm needles and one strand of wool or mohair, cast on 63 sts.

Work flower in coloured stripes for best effect.

Row 1: Knit.

Row 2: P1, p2tog, p1, p2togtbl, *p3, p2tog, p1, p2togtbl; rep from * to last st, p1. (47 sts)

Row 3: *Skpo, k1, k2tog, k1; rep from * to last 5 sts, skpo, k1, k2tog. (31 sts)

Row 4: P3tog, *p1, p3tog; rep from * to the end of the row. (15 sts)

Row 5: Sk2po, *k1, sk2po; rep from * to the end of the row. (7 sts)

Leaving a 40cm/15 in. tail, cut yarn. Thread tail through rem sts and pull up tightly.

Thread tail into knitter's sewing needle and join seam to complete flower.

Leaf cluster

Using 8mm needles and one strand of wool or mohair, cast on 15 sts.

Row 1: *Cast off 14 sts, slip rem st onto the left-hand needle, cast on 14 sts; *rep from * two or three more times. Leaving a 50cm/20 in. tail, cut yarn and fasten off.

The Noro Kureyon yarn knits up to give a striped effect, so for this bag I blended it with one strand of pure wool yarn to get a more subtle variegated effect.

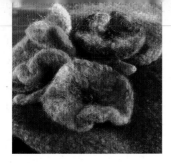

To make up

Using tails of yarn and following the photograph for position, sew the leaves and flowers in a group to the front of the bag. You can sew a decorative bead into the centre of each flower if you wish.

Measure the space between the slots in the bag handles and mark the positions with pins on the inside of the top of the bag. Thread the knitter's sewing needle or bodkin with one strand of A and sew one narrow end of a strip to each marked point, about 1cm/¼ in. down from the top edge. Thread the strips through the slots in the plastic handles. Sew the other narrow end of each strip to the inside of the bag, about 1cm/¼ in. below the first end.

Wrap the plastic handles tightly in bubble wrap and, with the bag right side out, fold the handles into the inside of the bag; this will protect them during the felting process in the washing machine. Close the bag opening with a safety pin or something similar to stop the handles from falling out.

If you want to use a wooden, beaded or bamboo handle that cannot be put through the wash cycle, then sew one end of each strip in place as described. Felt the bag, then thread the felted strips through the slots and sew the free ends in place.

Darn in all loose ends.

Following the instructions on pages 123–124, machine-wash the bag to felt it.

You can sew on a large snap fastener or press stud to fasten the bag if desired.

rust stripe bag

This bag is knitted following the pattern for the Variegated Stripe Bag, but using Knitting4fun Pure Wool in Rust for A and Noro Kureyon 201 for B. The flowers are worked in toning pure wools and leftover Noro Kureyon.

half bobble bag

You will need

- 150g of Knitting4fun Natural Merino Pure Wool in Light Grey (A)
- 150g of Knitting4fun Natural Merino Pure Wool in Dark Grey (B)
- 8mm (60cm/24 in. long) circular needle
- 10mm (60cm/24 in. or 80cm/32 in. long) circular needle
- Two 10mm double-pointed needles
- Knitter's sewing needle or bodkin for sewing
- Large snap fastener or press stud (optional)

Finished size

Bag measures approx 25cm/10 in. high by 29cm/11½ in. wide.

My bobble addiction crept in again with this bag, but maybe I wasn't fully bobble crazy that day, as I made half the bag plain and only half with bobbles.

I chose these colours to go with a particular outfit, but this is a bag design that looks fantastic knitted in any two shades of one colour, two toning colours, or, if you are feeling bold, in two clashing colours. Imagine it in chocolate brown and turquoise or in fuchsia pink and bright orange.

The handles for this bag are knitted i-cords, but to complement the bobble theme, the ends are tied in knots and pushed through the knitted bag fabric before felting. The knitting felts tightly around the base of the handles and the knots felt into chunky bobbles, which look great.

Tension

12 stitches and 14 rows to 10cm/4 in. over st st on 10mm needles using two strands of A held together, although tension is not crucial in felting.

Abbreviations

MB = make bobble: with two strands of contrast colour (k1, p1, k1) into next st, turn p3, turn k3, turn p3, turn sk2po, slip the stitch back onto the left-hand needle and knit into it again using main colour; cut contrast yarn, pull ends of contrast yarn tight to form the bobble, knot ends together and sew them into the back of the bobble before felting. Alternatively, strand contrast colour on the wrong side between bobbles and cut yarn at the end of each bobble row.

See also page 125.

Bag

Using 8mm circular needle and two strands of A held together, cast on 80 sts.

Join the cast on row into a circle, ensuring that the knitting is not twisted, and place a marker to establish the beginning of the round.

Round 1: [K1, p1] to the end of the row.

Round 2: [P1, k1] to the end of the row.

Rep rounds 1–2 once more then rep round 1 once more.

On the last row, mark the positions of the handles with four safety pins, placing them 10 sts, 30 sts, 50 sts and 70 sts from the marker.

Round 6: [K19, inc] four times. (84 sts)

Change to 10mm circular needle and cont in knit stitch.

Knit 7 rounds.

Shape sides

Slip marker to the right-hand needle and start the shaping as folls:

Round 14: K4, M1, k34, M1, k8, M1, k34, M1, k4. (88 sts)

Knit 7 rounds.

Round 22: K5, M1, k34, M1, k10, M1, k34, M1, k5. (92 sts)

Knit 3 rounds.

Break A and join in 2 strands of B.

Knit 2 rounds.

Round 27: K6, M1, k34, M1, k12, M1, k34, M1, k6. (96 sts)

Round 28 (bobble round): [K7, MB] to the end of the row.

Knit 6 rounds.

Round 34 (bobble round): K4 [MB, k7] to last 4 sts, MB, k3.

Knit 6 rounds.

Round 41 (bobble round): As round 28.

Knit 6 rounds.

Round 48 (bobble round): As round 34.

Knit 6 rounds.

Round 55 (bobble round): As round 28.

Knit 5 rounds.

Shape base

Slip marker to the right-hand needle and start the shaping as folls:

Round 61: K5, k2tog, k34, k2togtbl, k10, k2tog, k34, k2togtbl, k5. (92 sts)

Round 62: K4, k2tog, k34, k2togtbl, k8, k2tog, k34, k2togtbl, k4. (88 sts)

Round 63: K3, k2tog, k34, k2togtbl, k6, k2tog, k34, k2togtbl, k3. (84 sts)
Round 64: K2, k2tog, k34, k2togtbl, k4, k2tog, k34, k2togtbl, k2. (80 sts)
Round 65: K1, k2tog, k34, k2togtbl, k2, k2tog, k34, k2togtbl, k1. (76 sts)
Round 66: K2tog, k34, k2togtbl, k2tog, k34, k2togtbl. (72 sts)

Join base

Turn the bag inside out and push 36 sts along to each needle point. Put both needle points together and, using another knitting needle (the same size as the circular needle or a size larger), knit tog the first st on each needle point. Knit tog the second st on each needle point, then slip the first st over the second st, so casting off (not too tightly) and joining the base of the bag at the same time. Rep until all sts are cast off.

Handles (make two)

Using 10mm double-pointed needles and two strands of B held together, cast on 4 sts.

Knit 1 row.

Switch needles in your hands, so the needle with the stitches on is in your left hand again. Slide the stitches to the other end of the needle and, pulling the yarn across the back of the stitches, knit the row again. The first three or four rows will be flat but don't worry, after that the knitting will become tubular. Before knitting the first stitch of each row, give the yarn a tug to make the strand across the back disappear.

Cont in this way, sliding and knitting, until the handle is the required length. As the handles will shrink by approximately one-third during felting, I usually knit about 50–60 rows for a short hand-held handle, 100 rows for a longer hand-held handle and 120–140 rows for a shoulder handle.

Cast off.

To make up

Thread the ends of the handles through the knitting at the point marked by the safety pins, about 5 rows down from the top edge. Tie the ends in a tight knot on the right side. Using the knitter's sewing needle and one strand of D, sew through the knots, sewing them to the knitting so that they don't move during the felting process.

Darn in all loose ends.

Following the instructions on pages 123–124, machine-wash the bag to felt it.

You can sew on a large snap fastener or press stud to fasten the bag if desired.

My bobble addiction crept in again with this bag, but maybe I wasn't fully bobble crazy that day, as I made half the bag plain and only half with bobbles.

violets are blue

You will need

- 250g of Knitting4fun Pure Wool in Black (A)
- Small amounts of Knitting4fun Pure Wool in Purple, Damson and Apple Green
- Small amount of Knitting4fun Space-dyed Pure Wool in Purple
- Small amounts of Knitting4fun Fine Pure Wool in Lavender and Yellow
- 8mm (40cm/16 in. or 60cm/24 in. long) circular needle
- 10mm (60cm/24 in. or 80cm/32 in. long) circular needle
- Pair of 6mm knitting needles
- Pair of 8mm knitting needles
- Pair of plastic bag handles
- Knitter's sewing needle or bodkin for sewing
- Large snap fastener or press stud (optional)
- Decorative beads (optional)

This bag was inspired by the most perfect little black evening dress that I saw in a boutique. I wanted to make a black bag to go with it and knitted a variety of flowers in different shades of lavender, purple and violet to embellish the bag.

Some of the flowers are sewn straight onto the bag, but a couple of the larger ones are sewn onto brooch backs. This means that I can wear them as a corsage on the dress to match it beautifully with the bag.

This has been one of the most popular of my bags and I have knitted several versions with different-coloured flowers. On the Roses Are Red bag (see page 100) I used black crystal beads to decorate the centres of the flowers and add a bit of bling!

Choose yarn colours that match or complement your outfit to make your own version of this bag and decorate the flowers with beads or simple embroidery stitches, whichever you prefer.

Finished size

Bag measures approx
23cm/9 in. high by
29cm/11½ in. wide.

Tension

12 stitches and 14 rows to
10cm/4 in. over st st on
10mm needles using two
strands of A held together,
although tension is not crucial
in felting.

Abbreviations

See page 125.

Bag

Using 8mm circular needle and two strands of A held together, cast on 80 sts.

Join the cast on row into a circle, ensuring that the knitting is not twisted, and place a marker to establish the beginning of the round.

Round 1: [K1, p1] to the end of the row.

Round 2: [P1, k1] to the end of the row.

Rep rounds 1–2 twice more.

Round 7: [K19, inc] four times. (84 sts)

Change to 10mm circular needle and cont in knit stitch.

Knit 10 rounds.

Shape sides

Slip marker to the right-hand needle and start the shaping as folls:

Round 18: K4, M1, k34, M1, k8, M1, k34, M1, k4. (88 sts)

Knit 10 rounds.

Round 29: K5, M1, k34, M1, k10, M1, k34, M1, k5. (92 sts)

Knit 10 rounds.

Round 39: K6, M1, k34, M1, k12, M1, k34, M1, k6. (96 sts)

Knit 15 rounds.

Shape base

Slip marker to the right-hand needle and start the shaping as folls:

Round 55: K6, k2tog, k32, k2togtbl, k12, k2tog, k32, k2togtbl, k6. (92 sts)

Round 56: K5, k2tog, k32, k2togtbl, k10, k2tog, k32, k2togtbl, k5. (88 sts)

Round 57: K4, k2tog, k32, k2togtbl, k8, k2tog, k32, k2togtbl, k4. (84 sts)

Round 58: K3, k2tog, k32, k2togtbl, k6, k2tog, k32, k2togtbl, k3. (80 sts)

Round 59: K2, k2tog, k32, k2togtbl, k4, k2tog, k32, k2togtbl, k2. (76 sts)

Round 60: K1, k2tog, k32, k2togtbl, k2, k2tog, k32, k2togtbl, k1. (72 sts)

Round 61: K2tog, k32, k2togtbl, k2tog, k32, k2togtbl. (68 sts)

Join base

Turn the bag inside out and push 34 sts along to each needle point. Put both needle points together and, using another knitting needle (the same size as the circular needle or a size larger), knit tog the first st on each needle point. Knit tog the second st on each needle point, then slip the first st over the second st, so casting off (not too tightly) and joining the base of the bag at the same time. Rep until all sts are cast off.

Handle tabs (make four)

Using 8mm needles and one strand of A, cast on 4 sts.

Knit 8 rows.

Cast off.

Large flower

Using one strand of pure wool and 6mm knitting needles, cast on 11 sts.

Row 1: Knit 10 sts, turn.

Row 2: Sl1, k8, turn.

Row 3: Sl1, k7, turn.

Row 4: Sl1, k6, turn.

Row 5: Sl1, k5, turn.

Row 6: Sl1, k4, turn.

Row 7: Sl1, k3, turn.

Row 8: Sl1, knit to the end of the row.

Row 9: Sl1, k1 psso, then cast off all sts.

Leave rem st on needle and cast on 10 more sts. (11 sts)

Rep rows 1–9 four or five times more to give five or six petals, as desired.

Leaving a 50cm/20 in. tail, cut yarn. Thread knitter's sewing needle or bodkin with tail and sew through the edge of each petal and gather up, pulling the petals into a ring. Sew through the centre to hold the flower together.

Small flower

Using one strand of pure wool and 6mm knitting needles, cast on 9 sts.

Row 1: Knit 8 sts, turn.

Row 2: Sl1, k6, turn.

Row 3: Sl1, k5, turn.

Row 4: Sl1, k4, turn.

Row 5: Sl1, k3, turn.

Row 6: Sl1, knit to the end of the row.

Row 7: Sl1, k1 psso, then cast off all sts.

Leave rem st on needle and cast on 8 more sts. (9 sts)

Rep rows 1–7 four or five more times to give five or six petals, as desired.

Finish as for Large Flower.

This bag was inspired by the most perfect little black evening dress that I saw in a boutique.

Daisy

Using one strand of pure wool and 6mm knitting needles, cast on 7 sts.

Row 1: *Cast off 6 sts, slip rem st onto the left-hand needle, cast on 6 sts; *rep from * five or six more times. Leaving a 50cm/20 in. tail, cut yarn. Thread knitter's sewing needle or bodkin with tail and sew through the edge of each petal and gather up, pulling the petals into a ring. Sew through the centre to hold the flower together.

Leaf cluster

Using one strand of pure wool and 6mm knitting needles, cast on 15 sts.

Row 1: *Cast off 14 sts, slip rem st onto the left-hand needle, cast on 14 sts; *rep from * two or three more times. Leaving a 50cm/20 in. tail, cut yarn and fasten off.

To make up

Using tails of yarn and following the photograph for position, sew the flowers and leaves in a group to the front of the bag. You can embroider the centre of each flower with a French knot or sew on a decorative bead.

Measure the space between the slots in the bag handles and mark the positions with pins on the inside of the top of the bag. Thread the knitter's sewing needle or bodkin with one strand of A and sew one narrow end of a strip to each marked point, about 1cm/¼ in. down from the top edge. Thread the strips through the slots in the plastic handles. Sew the other narrow end of each strip to the inside of the bag, about 1cm/¼ in. below the first end.

Wrap the plastic handles tightly in bubble wrap and, with the bag right side out, fold the handles into the inside of the bag; this will protect them during the felting process in the washing machine. Close the bag opening with a safety pin or something similar to stop the handles from falling out.

If you want to use a wooden, beaded or bamboo handle that cannot be put through the wash cycle, then sew one end of each strip in place as described.

Felt the bag, then thread the felted strips through the slots and sew the free ends in place.

Darn in all loose ends.

Following the instructions on pages 123–124, machine-wash the bag to felt it.

You can sew on a large snap fastener or press stud to fasten the bag if desired.

roses are red

Made in exactly the same way as Violets Are Blue, this bag rings the changes by using red instead of blue yarns for the flowers.

small floral bag

After a long winter, spring came at last and the early pansies, beautiful bulbs and primroses were all blooming in my garden. This bag was inspired by those lovely spring colours.

The bag is knitted in apple green pure wool and knitted with it is an acrylic yarn that has lots of fresh colours running through it. It is a slightly textured yarn and when felted, gives a bouclé effect.

The bag is a dainty size and is very quick and easy to make, ideal for a party. I've been known to knit one the day before I'm going out and to arrive at the party with a bag that is still just a tiny bit damp from the felting process.

The flowers, which are also very easy to make, are knitted using pure wool in a variety of colours. They are stitched in place and can be embellished by sewing a French knot or a bead into the centre. You can make as many or as few flowers as you wish and arrange them in groups or scatter them individually around the bag.

Bag

Using 8mm circular needle and one strand each of A and B held together, cast on
55 sts.

Join the cast on row into a circle, ensuring that the knitting is not twisted, and
place a marker to establish the beginning of the round.

Round 1: [K1, p1] to last st, k1.

Round 2: [P1, k1] to last st, p1.

Rep rounds 1–2 once more, then rep round 1 once more.

Round 6: [K10, inc] five times. (60 sts)

Change to 9mm circular needle and cont in knit stitch.

Knit 10 rounds.

Shape sides

Slip marker to the right-hand needle and start the shaping as folls:

Round 17: K3, M1, k24, M1, k6, M1, k24, M1, k3. (64 sts)

Knit 12 rounds.

Round 30: K4, M1, k24, M1, k8, M1, k24, M1, k4. (68 sts)

Knit 14 rounds.

Shape base

Slip marker to the right-hand needle and start the shaping as folls:

Round 58: K4, k2tog, k22, k2togtbl, k8, k2tog, k22, k2togtbl, k4. (64 sts)

Round 59: K3, k2tog, k22, k2togtbl, k6, k2tog, k22, k2togtbl, k3. (70 sts)

Round 60: K2, k2tog, k22, k2togtbl, k4, k2tog, k22, k2togtbl, k2. (56 sts)

Round 61: K1, k2tog, k22, k2togtbl, k2, k2tog, k22, k2togtbl, k1. (52 sts)

Round 62: K2tog, k22, k2togtbl, k2tog, k22, k2togtbl. (48 sts)

Join base

Turn the bag inside out and push 24 sts along to each needle point. Put both needle
points together and, using another knitting needle (the same size as the circular
needle or a size larger), knit tog the first st on each needle point. Knit tog the
second st on each needle point, then slip the first st over the second st, so casting
off (not too tightly) and joining the base of the bag at the same time. Rep until all sts
are cast off.

Handles (make two)

Using 9mm double-pointed needles and two strands of A held together, cast on
4 sts.

Knit 1 row.

Switch needles in your hands, so the needle with the stitches on is in your left hand
again. Slide the stitches to the other end of the needle and, pulling the yarn across
the back of the stitches, knit the row again. The first three or four rows will be flat but
don't worry, after that the knitting will become tubular. Before knitting the first stitch
of each row, give the yarn a tug to make the strand across the back disappear.

Cont in this way, sliding and knitting, until the handle is the required length. As the
handles will shrink by approximately one-third during felting, I usually knit about
50–60 rows for a short hand-held handle, 100 rows for a longer hand-held handle
and 120–140 rows for a shoulder handle.

Cast off.

Flower

Using one strand of pure wool and 5mm knitting needles, cast on 7 sts.
Row 1: *Cast off 6 sts, slip rem st onto the left-hand needle, cast on 6 sts; *rep from
* five or six more times. Leaving a 50cm/20 in. tail, cut yarn. Thread knitter's sewing
needle or bodkin with tail and sew through the edge of each petal and gather up,
pulling the petals into a ring. Sew through the centre to hold the flower together.

To make up

Using tails of yarn and following the photograph for position, sew the flowers to the
front of the bag. You can sew a decorative bead or embroider a French knot into the
centre of each flower.

Using the knitter's sewing needle and A, sew the free end of the handle to the
opposite top edge of the bag.

Darn in all loose ends.

Following the instructions on pages 123–124, machine-wash the bag to felt it.

You can sew on a large snap fastener or press stud to fasten the bag if desired.

After a long winter, spring came at last and the early pansies, beautiful bulbs and primroses were all blooming in my garden.

pom-pom perfect

- 200g of Knitting4fun Pure Wool in Fuchsia (A)
- 150g of Knitting4fun Pure Wool in Lavender (B)
- 50g of Crystal Palace Yarns Popcorn in Violet Plums 442 (C)
- 50g of Knitting4fun Pure Wool in Purple (D)
- 8mm (60cm/24 in. long) circular needle
- 10mm (60cm/24 in. or 80cm/32 in. long) circular needle
- Two 10mm double-pointed needles
- Pair of 8mm knitting needles
- Button or toggle for fastening
- Knitter's sewing needle or bodkin for sewing

Finished size

Bag measures approx 25cm/10 in. high by 30cm/12 in. wide.

I found this amazing popcorn yarn and just had to have a ball of it – in the same way as I had to have the hundreds of other yarns that I have stashed away around the house.

Having made the grey Half Bobble Bag (see page 92), I liked the idea of half the bag in one colour and the other half in another colour. Using the popcorn yarn in a textured band around the middle divided and balanced the plain colours and was the perfect way to use up my one ball.

The knotted handles and the tab for the button closure are knitted in a third colour, picked out from the popcorn yarn.

This design lends itself to being made in many different colourways, as there are so many pom-pom and popcorn yarns in such wonderful colour combinations. Alternatively, the popcorn yarn could be added in rows randomly as you knit the bag, with just one main colour of pure wool used throughout.

Tension

12 stitches and 14 rows to 10cm/4 in. over st st on 10mm needles using two strands of A held together, although tension is not crucial in felting.

Abbreviations

See page 125.

Bag

Using 8mm circular needle and two strands of A held together, cast on 80 sts.

Join the cast on row into a circle, ensuring that the knitting is not twisted, and place a marker to establish the beginning of the round.

Round 1: [K1, p1] to the end of the row.

Round 2: [P1, k1] to the end of the row.

Rep rounds 1–2 once more, then rep round 1 once more.

On the last row, mark the positions of the handles with four safety pins, placing them 10 sts, 30 sts, 50 sts and 70 sts from the marker.

Round 6: [K19, inc] four times. (84 sts)

Change to 10mm circular needle and cont in knit stitch.

Knit 12 rounds.

Shape sides

Slip marker to the right-hand needle and start the shaping as folls:

Round 19: K4, M1, k34, M1, k8, M1, k34, M1, k4. (88 sts)

Knit 6 rounds.

Cut A and join in 1 strand each of B and C.

Purl 6 rounds. Purling the stitches helps to keep the textured yarn on the right side of the knitting.

Cut C and join in a second strand of B.

Round 32: K5, M1, k34, M1, k10, M1, k34, M1, k5. (92 sts)

Knit 12 rounds.

Round 45: K6, M1, k34, M1, k12, M1, k34, M1, k6. (96 sts)

Knit 17 rounds.

Shape base

Slip marker to the right-hand needle and start the shaping as folls:

Round 63: K6, k2tog, k32, k2togtbl, k12, k2tog, k32, k2togtbl, k6. (92 sts)

Round 64: K5, k2tog, k32, k2togtbl, k10, k2tog, k32, k2togtbl, k5. (88 sts)

Round 65: K4, k2tog, k32, k2togtbl, k8, k2tog, k32, k2togtbl, k4. (84 sts)

Round 66: K3, k2tog, k32, k2togtbl, k6, k2tog, k32, k2togtbl, k3. (80 sts)

Round 67: K2, k2tog, k32, k2togtbl, k4, k2tog, k32, k2togtbl, k2. (76 sts)

Round 68: K1, k2tog, k32, k2togtbl, k2, k2tog, k32, k2togtbl, k1. (72 sts)

Round 69: K2tog, k32, k2togtbl, k2tog, k32, k2togtbl. (68 sts)

Join base

Turn the bag inside out and push 34 sts along to each needle point. Put both needle points together and, using another knitting needle (the same size as the circular needle or a size larger), knit tog the first st on each needle point. Knit tog the second st on each needle point, then slip the first st over the second st, so casting off (not too tightly) and joining the base of the bag at the same time. Rep until all sts are cast off.

Flap

Using 8mm knitting needles and one strand of D, pick up 14 sts evenly along one top edge between safety pins.

Knit 16 rows.

Row 17: K2togtbl, k10, k2tog. (12 sts)

Row 18: K4, cast off 4 sts, knit to the end of the row. (8 sts)

Row 19: K2togtbl, k2, cast on 3 sts, k2, k2tog. (9 sts)

Row 20: Knit.

Row 21: K2togtbl, k5, k2tog. (7 sts)

Cast off.

Handles (make two)

Using 10mm double-pointed needles and two strands of D held together, cast on 4 sts.

Knit 1 row.

Switch needles in your hands, so the needle with the stitches on is in your left hand again. Slide the stitches to the other end of the needle and, pulling the yarn across the back of the stitches, knit the row again. The first three or four rows will be flat but don't worry, after that the knitting will become tubular. Before knitting the first stitch of each row, give the yarn a tug to make the strand across the back disappear.

Cont in this way, sliding and knitting, until the handle is the required length. As the handles will shrink by approximately one-third during felting, I usually knit about 50–60 rows for a short hand-held handle, 100 rows for a longer hand-held handle and 120–140 rows for a shoulder handle.

Cast off.

To make up

Thread the ends of the handles through the knitting at the point marked by the safety pins, about 5 rows down from the top edge. Tie the ends in a tight knot on the right side. Using the knitter's sewing needle and one strand of D, sew through the knots, sewing them to the knitting so that they don't move during the felting process.

Darn in all loose ends.

Following the instructions on pages 123–124, machine-wash the bag to felt it.

You can sew on a large snap fastener or press stud to fasten the bag if desired.

I found this amazing popcorn yarn and just had to have a ball of it – in the same way as I had to have the hundreds of other yarns that I have stashed away around the house.

yarns and techniques

The basic bag shapes are very easy to knit, so novice knitters can approach the projects with confidence. The felting process is equally simple, as the washing machine does all the hard work for you. You'll also find in this chapter all the information you need on choosing yarns for your bags.

choosing and using yarns

I knitted the bags in this book in a variety of yarns and each pattern tells you what I used to make the bag shown: turn to page 126 for suppliers. However, one of the wonderful things about felting is that you can experiment with yarns, so I have given ideas for substitutes if you want to try something different.

Yarns used

Here are specifications for all the yarns used in the bag patterns in this book. If you'd like to use different yarns, turn to pages 113–118 to find ideas and recommendations for substitute yarns.

- Knitting4fun Pure Wool, 100% pure wool, 100g/200m
- Knitting4fun Chunky Pure Wool, 100% pure wool, 100g/100m
- Knitting4fun Space-dyed Pure Wool, 100% pure wool, 100g/150m
- Knitting4fun Natural Merino Wool, 100% pure wool, 100g/200m
- Knitting4fun Fine Pure Wool, 100% pure wool, 100g/250m
- Knitting4fun Banana Fibre Kaleidoscope Yarn, 100% banana fibre, 200g/130–150m
- Knitting4fun Recycled Sari Silk Yarn, 100% silk, 200g/130–150m
- Colinette Giotto, 50% cotton, 40% rayon, 10% nylon, 100g/144m
- Crystal Palace Yarns Popcorn, 100% nylon, 50g/67m
- Elle Pizzazz, 65% acrylic, 35% polyester, 50g/55m
- Filati FF Park, 68% polyester, 32% nylon, 50g/40m
- Ice Long Eyelash, 100% polyester, 50g/35m
- Ice Catena, 100% polyamide, 50g/100m
- Katia Cancan, 100% polyester, 50g/42m
- Lang Mille Colori, 50% new wool, 50% acrylic, 50g/100m (4)
- Noro Kureyon, 100% pure wool, 50g/92m

Substituting yarns

I have used my own Knitting4fun pure wool yarns throughout this book as, having tried and tested them many times, I know that they felt beautifully at 40 degrees in the washing machine and that they keep their colour. However, if you want to use a different yarn to a specified project yarn, here are some suggestions. I can't guarantee the results, but I have used these yarns to make felted projects.

Each bag knitting pattern will give the quantity of the yarn I have specified that is needed to knit it. However, you can't just buy the same quantity of the substitute yarn, as balls of different brands of yarn, even of the same type and ball weight, can contain different meterages of yarn. Check the meterage per ball of the specified pattern yarn (see the listing opposite) and multiply that figure by the quantity needed to establish the total meterage needed for the project, then buy the same meterage of the substitute yarn.

It is always a good idea to knit and felt a large swatch of a substitute yarn before knitting up a whole project (see Felting the Knitting, page 123). Keep notes on how the yarn felts and when you are happy with the result, go ahead and knit your project.

The substitute yarns

As a substitute for any of the Knitting4fun yarns you can try:

- Brown Sheep Company Inc, Top of the Lamb Worsted, 100% wool, 1 skein/173m
- Brown Sheep Company Inc, Lamb's Pride Worsted 85% wool, 15% mohair, 1 skein/173m
- Cascade Yarns, Cascade 220 Wool, 100% Peruvian wool, 100g/201m

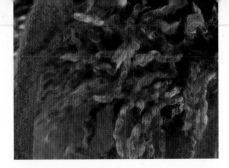

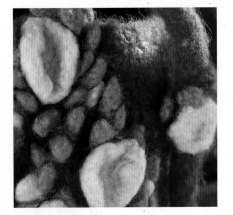

Pure purple

Plant pot

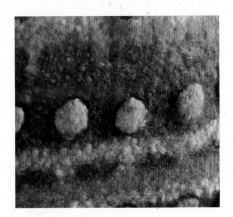

Flower power

Listed here are suggestions for substitutes for the fancy yarns used to make the bags. For substitutes for the Knitting4fun yarns, turn to page 113. There is such a huge range of yarns available that generally I have specified types rather than brands, so you are sure to find something suitable in your yarn shop.

PURE PURPLE, PAGE 10

Yarn used

- Knitting4fun Pure Wool in Purple and Damson, 100% pure wool, 100g/200m
- Elle Pizzazz in Poison 252, 65% acrylic, 35% polyester, 50g/55m

I used two toning shades of Knitting4fun Pure Wool to make a variegated colour to match colours in the Elle Pizzazz yarn.

Substitute yarn

Any eyelash yarn will work for the top edge, but the textures may be different.

PLANT POT, PAGE 14

Yarn used

- Knitting4fun Pure Wool in Rust, 100% pure wool, 100g/200m
- Colinette Giotto in Windfall 149, 50% cotton, 40% rayon, 10% nylon, 100g/144m
- Knitting4fun Pure Wool in Apple Green, Yellow and Cream, 100% pure wool, 100g/200m

Colinette Giotto gives texture and sheen once the bag is felted.

Substitute yarn

Any ribbon yarn will give a similar, though not identical, effect.

FLOWER POWER, PAGE 18

Yarn used

- Knitting4fun Pure Wool in Lime Green and Turquoise, 100% pure wool, 100g/200m
- Colinette Giotto in Lagoon 138, 50% cotton, 40% rayon, 10% nylon, 100g/144m

The mix of colours and yarns gives a tweedy look.

Substitute yarn

Any ribbon yarn will give a similar effect, as long as you choose the colour carefully.

PAINT BOX BAG, PAGE 22

Yarn used

- Knitting4fun Pure Wool, 100% pure wool, 100g/200m

It's the mix of vibrant colours make this bag so striking.

Substitute yarn

Choose a good range of strong colours in a substitute for Knitting4fun yarn.

JAZZY BAG, PAGE 30

Yarn used

- Knitting4fun Pure Wool in Turquoise, 100% pure wool, 100g/200m
- Elle Pizzazz in Carnival 253, 65% acrylic, 35% polyester, 50g/55m
- Ice Long Eyelash in Fuchsia, 100% polyester, 50g/35m

I love the heavily textured, dreadlock-type fronds of the Elle Pizzazz yarn.

Substitute yarn

Any mix of eyelash yarns will create a fluffy top edge.

Paint box bag

Jazzy bag

JAZZY BOOK BAG, PAGE 34

Yarn used

- Knitting4fun Pure Wool in Turquoise, 100% pure wool, 100g/200m
- Filati FF Park in colour 45, 68% polyester, 32% nylon, 50g/40m
- Ice Catena in Aqua/Green/Blue, 100% polyamide, 50g/100m

The pom-pom yarn makes a thick, spongy fabric to help protect a laptop.

Substitute yarn

Use any eyelash, pom-pom, or popcorn yarns for this bag.

ORANGE FLUFF AND BOBBLE, PAGE 36

Yarn used

- Knitting4fun Natural Merino Wool in Grey, 100% pure wool, 100g/200m
- Ice Long Eyelash in Orange 8814, 100% polyester, 50g/35m
- Knitting4fun Pure Wool in Orange, 100% pure wool, 100g/200m

The Ice Long Eyelash yarn gives a thick, luxurious trim to the top of the bag.

Substitute yarn

Any eyelash yarn will work: the longer and thicker it is, the better the effect.

ANYTHING GOES STASH BAG, PAGE 40

Yarn used

- Knitting4fun Pure Wool, 100% pure wool, 100g/200m
- Any eyelash, feather, or ribbon yarns

This is a stash-busting bag design.

Substitute yarn

Any leftover eyelash, feather, ribbon, or other textured yarns.

RETRO BUTTON BAG, PAGE 46

Yarn used

- Knitting4fun Pure Wool in Brown, 100% pure wool, 100g/200m
- Katia Cancan in Brown, 100% polyester, 50g/42m

The Katia Cancan yarn has a long double eyelash and gives a very fluffy top edge.

Substitute yarn

Any long eyelash yarn will work well.

SLIP STITCH HONEYCOMB, PAGE 50

Yarn used

- Knitting4fun Pure Wool in Fuchsia and Orange, 100% pure wool, 100g/200m
- Ice Long Eyelash in Fuchsia and Orange, 100% polyester, 50g/35m

Knitting alternate rows of each colour of Ice Long Eyelash gives a variegated trim.

Substitute yarn

Any two colours of eyelash yarn will work for the fluffy top edge.

Jazzy book bag

Orange fluff and bobble

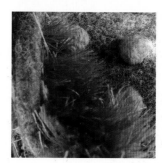

Anything goes stash bag

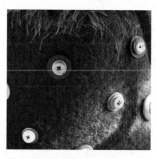

Retro button bag

Slip stitch honeycomb

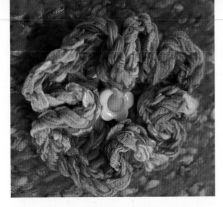

Red wool and ribbon

Cherry ripe

Recycled sari silk bag
Banana fibre bag

RED WOOL AND RIBBON, PAGE 56

Yarn used

- Knitting4fun Pure Wool in Red, 100% pure wool, 100g/200m
- Colinette Giotto in Fire 71, 50% cotton, 40% rayon, 10% nylon, 100g/144m

This bag makes good use of the tweedy effect the Colinette yarn produces when felted with a pure wool yarn.

Substitute yarn

You can use any ribbon yarn to create a similar effect.

CHERRY RIPE, PAGE 60

Yarn used

- Knitting4fun Natural Merino Wool in Dark Grey and Light Grey, 100% pure wool, 100g/200m
- Knitting4fun Space-dyed Pure Wool in Red and Green, 100% pure wool, 100g/150m

The space-dyed wool gives very subtle colour changes to the cherries and leaves, making them look more realistic.

Substitute yarn

You can try using either Crystal Palace Yarns Fjord Print Worsted Wool or South West Trading, Karaoke Multi Wool Blend.

RECYCLED SARI SILK BAG, PAGE 66

Yarn used

- Knitting4fun Pure Wool in Fuchsia, 100% pure wool, 100g/200m
- Knitting4fun Recycled Sari Silk Yarn, 100% silk, 200g/130–150m

The lovely bright colours in the Knitting4fun wool yarns match the bright colours in the recycled sari silk yarn.

Substitute yarn

You can use any recycled sari silk yarn for a similar effect.

BANANA FIBRE BAG, PAGE 70

Yarn used

- Knitting4fun Pure Wool in Violet, 100% pure wool, 100g/200m
- Knitting4fun Banana Fibre Kaleidoscope Yarn, 100% banana fibre, 200g/130–150m

The banana fibre yarn is another that works well with the colours of the Knitting4fun wool yarns.

Substitute yarn

You can use any banana fibre yarn for a similar effect.

Little saddle bag

LITTLE SADDLE BAG, PAGE 72

Yarn used

- Knitting4fun Pure Wool in Deep Pink, 100% pure wool, 100g/200m
- Lang Mille Colori in colour 65, 50% new wool, 50% acrylic, 50g/92m

The pure wool yarn traps the Mille Colori yarn and gives a slightly bouclé effect once felted.

Substitute yarn

You can try using either Crystal Palace Yarns Fjord Print Worsted Wool or South West Trading, Karaoke Multi Wool Blend.

ACORN AND OAK LEAF, PAGE 76

Yarn used

- Knitting4fun Pure Wool in Apple Green, Gold and Brown 100% pure wool, 100g/200m
- Knitting4fun Space-dyed Pure Wool in Green, 100% pure wool, 100g/150m
- Noro Kureyon in colour 201, 100% pure wool, 50g/100m

Mixing the Kureyon with the plain-colour wool yarn gives a more subtle effect to the striping of the Noro yarn and gives a firmer felt than if the Noro Kureyon is used alone.

Substitute yarn

You can try using any pure wool variegated yarn with a plain-coloured pure wool yarn.

MONOCHROME JAZZ, PAGE 82

Yarn used

- Knitting4fun Pure Wool in black, 100% pure wool, 100g/200m
- Elle Pizzazz in Zest 250, 65% acrylic, 35% polyester, 50g/55m
- Ice Long Eyelash in Black 7711, 100% polyester, 50g/35m

The mix of the Pizzazz yarn and Long Eyelash yarn create a really textural trim around the top of the bag.

Substitute yarn

You can mix any two types of eyelash yarn to create a similar, though not identical, effect.

VARIEGATED STRIPE BAG, PAGE 86

Yarn used

- Knitting4fun Pure Wool in Jade, 100% pure wool, 100g/200m
- Noro Kureyon in colour 173, 100% pure wool, 50g/100m

You can alter the look of a variegated yarn by knitting it together with a plain colour that picks up some of the tones in the multi-coloured yarn.

Substitute yarn

You can try using any pure wool variegated yarn with a plain-coloured pure wool yarn.

Acorn and oak leaf

Monochrome jazz bag

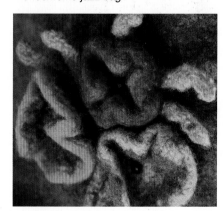

Variegated stripe bag

Half bobble bag

Violets are blue

Small floral bag

HALF BOBBLE BAG, PAGE 92

Yarn used

- Knitting4fun Natural Merino Wool in Light Grey and Dark Grey, 100% pure wool, 100g/200m

Mixing two shades of grey creates this understated yet sophisticated look.

Substitute yarn

Choose two shades of one colour in a pure wool yarn to get this effect.

VIOLETS ARE BLUE, PAGE 96

Yarn used

- Knitting4fun Pure Wool in Black, Purple, Damson and Apple Green, 100% pure wool, 100g/200m
- Knitting4fun Space-dyed Pure Wool in Purple, 100% pure wool, 100g/150m
- Knitting4fun Fine Pure Wool in Lavender and Yellow, 100% pure wool, 100g/250m

The space-dyed yarn gives the flowers subtle colour variations that make the most of the simple shapes.

Substitute yarn

You can try using either Crystal Palace Yarns Fjord Print Worsted Wool or South West Trading, Karaoke Multi Wool Blend.

SMALL FLORAL BAG, PAGE 102

Yarn used

- Knitting4fun Pure Wool in Apple Green, Purple, Orange and Yellow, 100% pure wool, 100g/200m
- Ice Catena in colour 6513, 100% polyamide, 50g/100m

The Ice Catena is a ladder-type yarn so when it is combined with pure wool and felted, the wool traps the acrylic yarn and creates a bouclé effect on the surface.

Substitute yarn

You could use any ladder-type yarn mixed with a pure wool yarn to get a similar effect.

POM-POM PERFECT, PAGE 106

Yarn used

- Knitting4fun Pure Wool in Fuchsia, Purple and Lavender, 100% pure wool, 100g/200m
- Crystal Palace Yarns Popcorn in Violet Plums 442, 100% nylon, 50g/67m

I love the texture and colours of the Popcorn yarn and they were easy to match with colours from the Knitting4fun range.

Substitute yarn

You can use any pom-pom or popcorn yarn for this bag.

Pom-pom perfect

handles, beads and buttons

Quite a few of my knitted and felted bags have plastic handles and I have used both beads and buttons as embellishments. Suppliers for all of these items can be found on page 126.

I have used several different styles of handbag handles. They are made from durable plastic and come in a range of colours, shapes and sizes.

You can find handles in some quite unusual colours and patterns that will complement the yarn colours you choose.

The buttons I have used are from various sources. Some are buttons that I have collected over the years, others are ones that I sell through my website. There is a huge range of buttons available through the Internet and the ones you choose will make your bags unique.

It is lovely to use up some of your own button stash, buttons that have memories attached to them, rather than leaving them hidden away out of sight in a box.

The beads that I have used to embellish the flowers on some of the bags are size 11 and size 15 seed beads and Czech and Swarovski crystals in various sizes.

knitting the bags

The patterns in this book are not complicated, so even if you are a beginner knitter you should be able to knit yourself a bag. In fact, the felting process hides a multitude of sins – uneven tension, twisted stitches and even dropped stitches disappear – so beginners have very little to worry about.

Knitting with a circular needle

The bags in this book are all knitted on a circular needle. I love using this type of needle as I don't have to sew up seams to finish the bag. There are circular needles available in plastic, bamboo, wood, metal or resin, and it is really a matter of deciding which material you prefer to work with.

Some people seem to find using a circular needle difficult, but it is very easy provided the cord joining the two needle points is the correct length. If the cord is too short the stitches will be crammed together and will take every opportunity to jump off the needle tips. If the cord is too long, the stitches won't reach around from one needle point to the other. Each bag pattern tells you how long the cord needs to be, so make sure you get the right length when you buy your needle.

Once you have cast on the required number of stitches for the bag, they have to be spread evenly around the needle cord. When joining the stitches to knit the first round, you need to make sure that the row of cast on stitches is not twisted or the knitting will be twisted. This will mean having to start the project again.

Knit the first stitch quite tightly when joining the start and end of the cast on row. I wrap the tail from the cast on around the yarn I am about to work with so that it tightens up the first stitch and joins the ends securely.

Remember to slip a round marker onto the needle between the first and last stitches so that you can easily see where the beginning of the round is. This is necessary so that you can tell when you have knitted the required number of rounds, and to keep track of your position when you are decreasing.

You can buy plastic, metal and beaded round markers, but a loop of contrast-coloured yarn will work just as well. However, if you do use a yarn round marker, be careful not to knit it as though it were a stitch!

Getting to the marker gives you the opportunity to have a break, a cup of tea, or go to bed. Otherwise you may just keep knitting round, and round, and round…

The cast on is the top edge of the bag. To create a firm top edge, the first few rows are usually knitted on a smaller size circular needle than the main body of the bag. Often these first rows are worked in moss stitch to stop the edge curling. If the bag has a fluffy trim on the top edge, made with eyelash yarn, then the first few rows are purled to put more of the fibres on the right side.

I find knitting on circular needles almost hypnotic, as I get into a rhythm and feel that the knitted fabric is produced more quickly than if I work on straight needles.

You then change to a larger size needle for the main body of the bag, knitting every stitch on every round. However, rather than producing garter stitch – which is what would happen if you knitted every stitch on every row working with straight needles – when you knit every row on the circular needle, the fabric you make is stocking stitch.

Many of the bags use a three-needle cast off; this casts off and joins the base at the same time. This cast off edge almost disappears when the bag is felted, creating a virtually invisible seam.

Anyone who suffers from arthritis may find knitting with circular needles easier than with straight needles, as the weight of the knitting is on the cord in your lap rather than on your wrists.

I find knitting on circular needles almost hypnotic, as I get into a rhythm and feel that the knitted fabric is produced more quickly than if I work on straight needles.

Circular needles are also more portable than longer straight needles, so you can happily knit on the bus or train without risk of poking your neighbour with the end of your knitting needle. If you have to stop for any reason, you can pull the ends of the needles up together and the work sits on the cord until you are ready to start again.

Knitting with double-pointed needles

Four or five double-pointed knitting needles are used to shape the base of some of the bags where there are not enough stitches to use a circular needle. The idea of knitting with more than two needles scares some people, but once you get the hang of it you will realise that you are still only using two needles at any given time; you can just ignore the ones that you aren't actually knitting with.

Double-pointed needles come in sets of four or five, which makes it easy to divide the stitches between the needles. You should have the same, or a similar, number of stitches on each working needle. With four needles, you divide the stitches between three of them and knit with the fourth. With five needles, you divide the stitches between four and knit with the fifth.

Usually, care has to be taken not to create a gap between the last stitch on one needle and the first stitch on the next, but for these bags this does not really matter so much, as the gaps will disappear once the piece is felted.

Two double-pointed needles are used for making the i-cord handles, as this is the quickest way to make the cords. I have used French knitting bobbins, but find using the double-pointed needles much quicker and more versatile as the number of stitches can be changed.

The felting process hides a multitude of sins – uneven tension, twisted stitches and even dropped stitches disappear.

felting the knitting

Once you have knitted your bag, you need to felt it. This isn't hard to do, as it's the washing machine that does the work for you. However, do read this section through and if you are using a substitute yarn (see page 113), knit and felt a swatch before making a bag.

The wool yarns that I use for the bags are pure merino wools that I import myself. They felt beautifully at 40 degrees to give a firm felt that holds its shape when dry. The yarns come in a wide range of colours and these colours can be knitted together to make yet more shades.

Because the wool yarns felt so well and so easily, other non-wool yarns can be knitted in with them and, providing the non-wool yarn is not thicker than the pure wool, it should felt well. The wool traps the non-wool yarn and still produces a firm enough felt to give the bag body. As the wool felts at 40 degrees, the acrylic yarns or non-wool yarns do not spoil, which they might do if they were felted at a higher temperature.

Being able to mix non-wool yarns with the pure wool allows you to add lots of texture and decoration. I have incorporated eyelash, feather, ribbon, sari silk, banana fibre, metallic and sequinned yarns and they all have worked beautifully.

Before felting, the knitted bag will look very much like an ugly duckling, but it will turn out to be a swan! The bag will be much larger than you would expect, but it will shrink by approximately one-third in length and one-quarter in the width. The handles will look very long, almost ridiculously long, but they will shrink quite dramatically and firm up once felted.

I prefer to sew most of the embellishments on before felting – so that they actually felt into the bag and become an integral part of it – rather than sewing them on afterward. Use pure wool yarn and a knitter's sewing needle or bodkin

As this pre-felted version of an Anything Goes Stash Bag (see page 40) shows, before it is felted the knitting will be enormous and very floppy. But don't worry, it'll change completely once felted.

to sew on the embellishments. If I use buttons as a closure then I sew them on with wool yarn so that they felt into the bag and make a strong, secure fastening. Sew on snap fasteners with wool yarn, too, and they will also felt into the bag. If the buttons are purely for decoration, I tend to sew them on after felting as they can move during the felting process.

Felting in the washing machine

This is where your floppy, huge, knitted thing turns into a gorgeous and practical felted bag.

I use a front-loading washing machine for felting my knitted bags. Choose a full 40 degree programme, rather than a short programme, as this gives the agitation needed to felt the bag. This agitation is very important, as it is this as well as the temperature that felts the wool. Some washing machines may need to be set at a higher temperature to get perfect results. The 40 degree programme turns the Knitting4fun yarns into a firm felt, which I like, but if you prefer a lighter felt, then you can experiment with shorter washes and different temperatures.

I do use laundry detergent and usually put the bag in an empty washing machine – rather than in with other items such as towels, jeans, or old trainers – as I think a bag felts better by itself. You can place the bag in an empty pillowcase to stop any fibres clogging up the filter, particularly when using mohair yarn. If you can open the filter easily it is best to clean it regularly so as not to clog it up and possibly cause damage to the washing machine.

Spin the bag dry then take it out of the washing machine as soon as possible. Do not allow the bag to sit in the machine for too long or creases may appear. If, after going through the wash programme, the bag has not felted enough, try putting it through again at the same temperature rather than at a higher temperature. If that does not work, then try a higher temperature. Once it is fully felted, the bag will shrink by about one-third in length and one-quarter in width. You must consider this shrinkage when designing your own bag patterns.

The bag will now need to be stretched into shape: I use tins or cartons to do this. You must shape the bag while it is damp as once it is dry it cannot be shaped without dampening it again. Place the tins in the damp bag so that the felt is taut and the bag is the desired shape. Leave the tins in the bag while it dries, placing it on the windowsill or a radiator. If the handles have shrunk a little too much, hang the bag from a radiator with the tins still inside so that the weight of them stretches the handles while they dry.

If the handles do not felt firmly enough, try holding the damp bag and hitting the handles against the wall outside the house. This seems to shock the wool and firms it up.

You can also do this to the body of the bag if it has not felted enough. Just be aware of the neighbours or the postman, as they will think you are crazy, beating your handbag against the wall.

If the felted bag seems a little too fluffy, which it can do occasionally, depending on the yarns that have been used (mohair or alpaca are very hairy), I sometimes use hair clippers to shave the bag. I often do this outside so that the birds can have the fibres for their nests. This is when the neighbours and postman do decide that I am completely crazy, because it's not every day you see a woman shaving her handbag on the doorstep!

I have not felted my bags by hand personally, but have had friends do this. You can wash the bag in warm water in a big saucepan and agitate it by stirring and by repeatedly throwing it into the sink to shock the wool. Rinse it under the cold tap and then the hot tap and keep throwing it into the sink or bashing it against the draining board, beating or 'fulling' it until it is firmly felted.

abbreviations and conversions

A, B, C	colours as listed
alt	alternate; alternatively
approx	approximately
cm	centimetre(s)
cont	continue
dc	double crochet
dec(s)	decrease(s)(ing)
foll(s)	follow(s)(ing)
g	gram(s)
inc	increase(s)(ing)
k	knit
k2tog	knit two stitches (or number stated) together
M1	make one stitch by picking up horizontal strand between stitches with tip of left-hand needle, using right-hand needle, knit into back of picked up strand
MB	make bobble
p	purl
p2tog	purl two stitches (or number stated) together
patt(s)	pattern(s)
psso	pass the slipped stitch over the stitch just worked
rem	remain(ing)
rep	repeat
RS	right side
skpo	slip one stitch, knit one stitch, pass slipped stitch over
sk2po	slip one stitch, knit two stitches together, pass slipped stitch over
sl	slip
st st	stocking stitch
st(s)	stitch(es)
tbl	through back of loop
tog	together
tr	treble crochet

Needle sizes

There are three systems of sizing needles and here are the equivalent sizes across all three.

Metric	US	old UK and Canadian
25	50	–
19	35	–
15	19	–
10	15	000
9	13	00
8	11	0
7.5	11	1
7	10½	2
6.5	10½	3
6	10	4
5.5	9	5
5	8	6
4.5	7	7
4	6	8
3.75	5	9
3.5	4	–
3.25	3	10
3	2/3	11
2.75	2	12
2.25	1	13
2	0	14
1.75	00	–
1.5	000	–

resources

There is a huge range of yarns available to today's knitter by mail order over the Internet. Here is a list of suppliers of the yarns I have used in this book. You will find that many of these websites also have details of worldwide stockists.

Suppliers of yarns

Knitting4fun is my own yarn company. It was set up because I struggled to find the yarns I wanted to use. I tend to sell natural-fibre yarns and pure wools or wool blends. Many of the yarns are also fair trade yarns, particularly from South America and Nepal. Come and visit us at the website and see what we are up to.
www.knitting4fun.com

The complete range of Brown Sheep yarns.
www.brownsheep.com

The complete range of Cascade yarns.
www.cascadeyarns.com

The complete range of Colinettte yarns.
www.colinette.com

The complete range of Crystal Palace yarns, including Fjord Print Worsted Wool.
www.crystalpalaceyarns.com

The complete range of Noro yarns.
www.designeryarns.uk.com

The complete range of Elle yarns.
www.elleyarnsuk.com

The complete range of Filati yarns.
www.filatiyarn.com

The complete range of Ice yarns.
www.iceyarns.com

The complete range of Katia yarns.
www.katia.ee

The complete range of Lang yarns.
www.langyarns.ch/en

Karaoke Multi Wool Blend yarn.
www.soysilk.com

Suppliers of plastic bag handles
www.joggles.com
www.karrydot.co.uk
www.u-handbag.com

Suppliers of buttons
www.buttoncompany.co.uk
www.buttonsunlimited.co.uk

Suppliers of beads
www.beadmerchant.co.uk
www.spellboundbead.co.uk

These are two of my favourite yarn companies; they supply great ranges of lovely yarns.
www.creativeyarns.co.uk
www.yarnparadise.com

This is my favourite supplier of wonderful fabrics, haberdashery and wools, and they also stock Knitting4fun yarns.
www.heathscountrystore.co.uk

index

A

Abbreviations 125
Acorn and oak leaf 76–81
Anything goes stash bag 40–43

B

Banana fibre bag 70–71
Bucket bags 8–27
    Flower power 18–21
    Paint box bag 22–27
    Plant pot 14–17
    Pure purple 10–13
Bunch of cherries 64–65

C

Cherry ripe 60–64
Choosing and using yarns 112–118
Conversions 125

F

Felting in the washing machine 124
Felting the knitting 123–124
Flat-bottomed bags 28–53
    Anything goes stash bag 40–43
    Jazzy bag 30–33
        Jazzy book bag 34–35
    Orange fluff and bobble 36–39
        Red fluff and bobble 39
    Retro button bag 46–49
        Rounded stash bag 44–45
    Slip stitch honeycomb 50–53
Flower power 18–21

H

Half bobble bag 92–95
Handles, beads and buttons 119

J

Jazzy bag 30–33
Jazzy book bag 34–34

K

Knitting the bags 120–122
Knitting with a circular needle 121–122
Knitting with double-pointed needles 122

L

Little saddle bag 72–75

M

Monochrome jazz 82–85

O

Orange fluff and bobble 36–39

P

Paint box bag 22–27
Plant pot 14–17
Pom-pom perfect 106–109
Pure purple 10–13

R

Recycled sari silk bag 66–69
Red fluff and bobble 39
Red wool and ribbon 56–59

Retro button bag 46–49
Roses are red 100–101
Rounded stash bag 44–45
Rust stripe bag 90–91

S

Shaped bags 54–109
    Acorn and oak leaf 76–81
        Banana fibre bag 70–71
        Bunch of cherries 64–65
    Cherry ripe 60–64
    Half bobble bag 92–95
    Little saddle bag 72–75
    Monochrome jazz 82–85
    Pom-pom perfect 106–109
    Recycled sari silk bag 66–69
    Red wool and ribbon 56–59
        Roses are red 100–101
        Rust stripe bag 90–91
    Small floral bag 102–105
    Variegated stripe bag 86–90
    Violets are blue 96–100
Slip stitch honeycomb 50–53
Small floral bag 102
Substituting yarns 113–118

V

Variegated stripe bag 86–90
Violets are blue 96–100

Y

Yarns and techniques 110–124

acknowledgments

This is my chance to say thank you to many of the people who have helped me along the way, but maybe they didn't realise they had.

My mother's godmother, Auntie Mo, and my grandmother, Ida, taught me knitting and crochet as a child, along with many other crafts, and my grandfather, Joe, used to buy me many of the materials I needed. I did not appreciate at the time how much he had encouraged me, too. Auntie Mo would take me into Nottingham and we would go into Bellman's yarn shop. There seemed to be a huge array of colours and little balls of wonderful yarns. I would be treated to some yarn and then to a drink and cake in a café. My yarn addiction started there, at such a young age.

I would like to thank my college tutors, Cherrilyn Tyler and Pauline Barke, who supported and encouraged me to explore my ideas and gave me the confidence to carry them out. Also Sandra Coleridge, whom I met through Valerie Campbell Harding when they were teaching together. They are all valued friends and mentors.

I would like to thank Jenny and Tanya for buying those first handbags from me when I certainly had no intention of selling my wares. My mum, Doreen, and sisters, Bernadette and Bridget, were great models for the bags and then became my sales team.

Thanks to Elaine and Julie, who gave me a job when I needed one, and for all their support and friendship.

My husband, Tom (Poor Tom, as he is now better known), and son, Frazer, who have had to suffer wool in almost every room in the house. Tom has been dragged (I think he enjoyed it really) to the knitting and yarn shows and has helped me tremendously, along with my mum and Karen and Gill.

I would like to thank all of the knitters I have met at our knitting groups, at shows, and over the Internet. Without you buying my patterns and kits I may not have ended up writing this book. We knitters come from all walks of life and knitting crosses generations: I have so many new friends, and hopefully many more to come, that I am grateful to knitting for that.

Thanks to Paula, Janet, Jane and all of the team at Breslich & Foss for asking me to produce this book.

Special thanks to Kate Haxell, my editor, Sussie Bell, the photographer, and Elizabeth Healey, the designer, for making this book come alive.

I want to take this opportunity to thank Dr Claire Joynson and all of the oncology team at Leicester Royal Infirmary for their medical care, help and support during my treatment for cancer. I was treated with respect, compassion, and importantly, as an individual. I truly felt that I had, and am still having, the best ever care. Many of the bags in this book were knitted during my stay at the hospital while undergoing the weeks of radiotherapy treatment.

As a foster carer I would also like to thank the children who have enriched our home over the past few years, some of you staying for only a few days and some of you for years. I will never forget you and have such fond memories. Many of you have also been introduced to the world of yarn and knitting by the mad wool woman with crazy coloured hair.